101 Ideas for the Best-Ever Christmas

101
Ideas for the
Best-Ever
Christmas

Caryl Waller Krueger

DIMENSIONS

FOR LIVING

NASHVILLE

101 IDEAS FOR THE BEST-EVER CHRISTMAS

This book is printed on recycled, acid-free paper.

Library of Congress Cataloging-in-Publication Data

Krueger, Caryl W., 1929–
    101 ideas for the best-ever Christmas   / Caryl Waller Krueger.
      p. cm.
    ISBN 0-687-29069-4
    1. Christmas.   I. Title.   II. Title: One hundred and one ideas for better-ever Christmas.
  III. Title: One hundred one ideas for better-ever Christmas.
GT4985.K64   1992
394.2'68282—dc20   92-4445
                                                                    CIP

Design by John R. Robinson

Illustrations by Tom Armstrong

Some of the ideas in this book are from the author's books *1001 Things to Do with Your Kids*, copyright © 1988 by Caryl Waller Krueger, published by Abingdon Press, Nashville, Tennessee 37203; and *Six Weeks to Better Parenting*, copyright 1985 by Pelican Publishing Company, Gretna, Louisiana 70053.

The author has made every effort to make the information and suggestions in this book practical and workable, but neither she nor the publisher assumes any responsibility for successes, failures, or other results of putting these ideas into practice.

MANUFACTURED IN THE UNITED STATES OF AMERICA

To Carrie with love
for the many ways she cares for others and
because she understands the true meaning of Christmas

Contents

Acknowledgments

Friends around the world helped to make this book possible. I'm especially grateful for the extensive information several shared on how Christmas is celebrated in other countries: Carolyn Schoenfeld (England), Berit Kinter (Sweden), Reynold and Evelyn Ramseyer (Switzerland), Sandy Vavra (Eastern Europe), and Robin and Karen Dornaus (Tasmania).

Also, my thanks to Sheila Kinder and Cliff Krueger for reading the manuscript, and to Myrna Bennett for help in compiling the bibliography. And I owe a debt of love to my parents, who, as Dickens said, "knew how to keep Christmas" and loved me enough to let me keep the dog named Boots.

Introduction

A Different Christmas

L ast-minute shopping, hasty tree trimming, frantic cooking, big bills to pay, short tempers—has that been the story of your Christmas season? If it's a chaotic, materialistic, expensive scramble, it really misses the point of celebrating the birth of Jesus. On the other hand, Christmas shouldn't be regimented and predictable so that there's no room for spontaneity.

Let me introduce you to the real joys of this holiday, a holiday based on God's great love for us—a love so great that God sent his Son to guide us. While this is not a book on the religious aspects of Christmas, it does include some nondenominational ideas that are the foundation for this best-ever holiday.

Love was the basis of Jesus' ministry and should be the foundation of our celebrations. The love that we share is not just for children, but for all the family, for those beyond the family circle, and for the entire world.

This book tells you how to turn the month of December into a real celebration of love. You will find many things you'll want to do, but don't try everything this year—save some ideas for the years to come. Remember that basic organization is necessary, but you still need to keep the joyful spontaneity of the holidays.

You'll find a step-by-step plan for getting all the routine things accomplished so that you will have time for outreach, inspiration, and family togetherness. At the same time, you'll find stories and activities to make your celebration this year the best-ever Christmas, the first of many, many to come.

So it's onward to a Merry Christmas!

Caryl Waller Krueger

How to Get Everything Done—
and Enjoy It!

"Gathering Christmas Greens." An illustration from c. 1876.

Chapter One

How to Get Everything Done—and Enjoy It!

Here's a short story that may sound familiar: Once upon a time there was a family who spent the entire month of December rushing about getting ready for Christmas. They complained continuously about all the work they had to do. They shopped with cranky children, argued the entire time they trimmed the Christmas tree, had no time for others who needed their love, mailed their Christmas cards on Christmas Eve, ripped open the packages Christmas morning, forgot to write thank-you notes, never mentioned Jesus' birth, and were exhausted by December 31.

If this story sounds even slightly like the goings-on at your house, this chapter will give you a simple outline that lets you enjoy the entire holiday season—and at the same time get the important things done on schedule. Of course, you'll alter this "calendar of things to do" to tie in with your own plans, but this chapter should give you some concrete ideas on how to have a memorable, stress-free Christmas.

Many of these ideas need more complete descriptions and have been cross-referenced to fuller details in other chapters in this book.

After Thanksgiving

1. **Use Dinner-time for Talk.** Discuss this holiday month with your family—everyone is eager to help when included in the planning. Don't try to do too much. Talk about good ideas from Christmases past.

2. **The Big December Calendar.** Put it where it can be seen often. Put in the dates you know—school and church programs, social events—and add to it. Make sure no day or week gets overloaded.

3. **Decide on Entertaining—or Not.** Will it be family only on Christmas Eve? Or maybe a caroling party for friends? Or a Christmas potluck with the neighbors? Mark dates for entertaining on your calendar, and mark out the time for sending invitations, party planning, and food preparation. That way you won't be rushed later. See chapter 5, "Sharing the Spirit," and chapter 3, "101 Ways to Make Christmas Memorable," ideas 49-58, for ideas on entertaining.

4. **Consider Buying a Crèche.** See chapter 8, "The Christmas Story at Your House," for the importance of the nativity scene in your celebration.

5. **Talk about the Christmas Family.** One of the greatest projects for the month of December is "adopting" a family. Complete details are in chapter 5.

6. **Wish Lists.** There will be Christmas gifts, and these gifts should reflect the interests and needs of each family member. So let each one make a list of wants, being sure to include both large and small items. (This list can be shared with relatives who need suggestions.) Encourage a variety of suggestions, including books, clothes, sports equipment, games, educational toys, art objects, wall hangings, and so forth.

7. Make Shopping Lists. From the wish lists, each person can make a shopping list. Put on the calendar for the next two weeks the times you will shop—two times alone, one time with the family. Siblings should plan to buy or make gifts for one another, for parents, and for grandparents. You may want to subsidize these gifts by paying a certain percentage of the price, depending on the age of the child. See chapter 3, idea 67.

8. Consider Homemade Gifts. Decide if there's time this year, or if it's better to wait until next Christmas and start the crafts next summer. Avoid the panic of finishing a knitting, woodworking, or painting project on Christmas Eve. For homemade gift items, see chapter 3, ideas 70-76.

9. Select Christmas Cards. If you haven't done so already, take the family along and pick out your cards. Don't have your name printed on them. It takes more time—besides, it's fun to personally sign them and add a message. Mark your calendar for a "Christmas Card Night" in the next two weeks. See chapter 3, ideas 59-65, for homemade cards.

10. Nostalgia Night. See chapter 3, idea 10.

4 Weeks Before Christmas

1. Start the Christmas Candle. See chapter 3, idea 1.

2. The Christmas Story. On Sunday of this week (and every Sunday in December), read part of the story of Jesus' birth. See chapter 8 for the biblical text. If you have a nativity set, use it as you read part of the story each week.

3. The Advent Calendar.

4. The Christmas Coffee Cake. Avoid the last-minute rush and let the kids make a special Christmas-morning coffee cake now. Try the One Pecan Coffee Cake (chap. 3, idea 77). (The person who gets the nut on Christmas morning can be the first to give gifts.) Wrap and freeze the coffee cake.

5. Christmas Angels. Don't miss this wonderful, easy-to-do activity in chapter 3, idea 3.

6. Select a Special Event. Look in the newspaper or school newsletter or church bulletin for a concert, program, or special event the entire family will enjoy. Consider a trip to the art museum to look at paintings of the birth of Jesus. Mark your calendar with the date.

7. Christmas Reading. See chapter 3, idea 2, and chapter 9, "Bibliography of the Best Christmas Literature."

8. Start Playing Christmas Music. Play recorded holiday music at dinner time. (When it is a carol, see who can name it first.) Encourage musical family members to learn to play some Christmas pieces.

9. Shopping with the Youngsters. Go in the early evening when stores are less crowded and the lights and decorations look beautiful. Let kids take the lead on this trip.

3 Weeks Before Christmas

This is the week to think about family and friends in faraway places. It's reach-out time across the miles.

1. The Christmas Story. See chapter 8.

2. Christmas Card Night. Everyone helps whether it is making cards, addressing, sealing, or stamping envelopes. If there is a mailbox nearby, mail them this very night. What a good feeling you'll have as you drop them in the box!

3. Christmas Shopping. On this trip, specialize in finding those gifts that must be mailed. Buy strapping tape and brown wrapping paper (or use inside-out grocery bags) and come home to wrap these

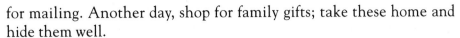

for mailing. Another day, shop for family gifts; take these home and hide them well.

4. Christmas Ornaments. While you are shopping, let the stay-at-homes make ornaments. See chapter 3, ideas 41-43.

5. Christmas Cookies. Make them now! First, make a deal with a friend that the two of you will each make a double batch of several kinds of cookies and then trade the extra batches, giving each of you greater variety with less work. For "Cookie Night" ideas and recipes, see chapter 3, ideas 4 and 80.

6. Christmas Family Update. If you have adopted a family, you'll need to set aside time this week to gather items and make your purchase list. See chapter 5 for ideas.

7. Decorate the House. See chapter 3, ideas 26-35.

8. Buy the Tree. See chapter 3, idea 36.

2 Weeks Before Christmas

You're making progress—and isn't it fun?

1. The Christmas Story. See chapter 8.

2. **An Important Phone Call.** Telephone a neighbor, relative, or shut-in to see how you can help with shopping, a meal, package wrapping or mailing, even selecting a tree.

3. **Special Gift Paper.** Let kids save you money by making their own wrapping paper. See chapter 3, idea 66.

4. **A Christmas Drive.** See chapter 3, idea 7.

5. **The Last Shopping Trip.** Absolutely finish shopping this week, remembering the things needed for the Christmas Family.

6. **The Ornament-of-the-Year.** See chapter 3, idea 40.

7. **Trim the Tree.** See chapter 3, ideas 44 and 47.

8. **Wrapping Day.** End the week with gift wrapping. See chapter 3, idea 68.

1 Week Before Christmas

'Twas the week before Christmas . . . the culmination of your organization plan. The cards are out, the house and tree are decorated, the packages are wrapped, and you're ready to share more of the meaning of Christmas with others. If you have planned a party with friends or neighbors, this is probably the week you will entertain. But don't let party work get in the way of family fun. If everyone helps, parties can be joyful times of sharing.

1. **The Christmas Story combined with Surprise Supper.** See chapter 8 and chapter 3, idea 50.

2. **The Star of Bethlehem.** See chapter 3, idea 8.

3. The Christmas Family. This is the week you'll gather the clothing and gift items and wrap them. See chapter 5 for details.

4. Out-of-Town Gifts. If you receive gifts from far away, consider opening some at dinner time each night. See chapter 3, idea 69.

5. Delivery Day. Everyone helps load the car with packages for the Christmas Family (see chapter 5 for details), cookies to deliver, and packages to take to family and friends. Don't forget little remembrances for the mail carrier and other service people. Sing carols in the car as you spread your cheer.

6. Telephone Night. At dinner, make a list of all relatives, senior citizens, and friends who would enjoy a holiday phone call. Divide the list among family members. Help each child think of something to share on the phone. Make some of the long distance calls tonight during an inexpensive calling time. Mark the calendar for a later date when you'll finish your calls.

7. The Christmas Movie. Go to a good one or rent a classic. Share the evening with friends.

8. The Christmas Cake. See chapter 3, idea 85.

9. Christmas Cooking and Entertaining. Be easy on yourself. Do a little each day. Try to prepare foods in advance, and even set the table in advance. See chapter 3, ideas 52-54.

Christmas Eve

1. The Christmas Story. Read the last part of the Christmas story as shared in chapter 8. You can do this even if you have guests at dinner.

2. **Christmas Angels.** Who has been doing good deeds for you this month? Let each person guess who was his or her Christmas angel and talk about the surprising things done. See chapter 3, idea 3.

3. **After-Supper Walk.** Go for a Christmas Eve stroll in the evening. Come back for hot chocolate and Christmas cookies.

4. **Christmas Eve at Church.** See chapter 3, idea 12.

5. **New PJs.** (This will require advance purchase.) See chapter 3, idea 13.

6. **Christmas Stocking Filling.** See chapter 3, idea 9.

7. **Breakfast Preparations.** Thaw the Christmas coffee cake made earlier in the month. Set out the napkins, dishes, flatware, and glasses wherever you plan to eat—the living room usually works best. Prepare a plate of Christmas cookies. Keep it simple because the morning will be busy!

Christmas Day

1. **Stockings and Breakfast.** See chapter 3, ideas 14 and 15.
2. **Opening the Gifts.** See chapter 3, idea 16.

3. **Take a stroll.** After the gifts have been opened, consider a walk around the block (see chapter 3, idea 17)—or even a short nap. Kids who think they don't need a nap can curl up in front of a TV special with their favorite new toy (and many will fall asleep). There may be visits or a dinner or other festivities this day, so everyone needs to be ready.

4. Going Out. If you're going out today, let everyone, kids and adults, take along one gift to show or share, or wear a new piece of clothing. See if those you're visiting can recognize what's new.

5. Bedtime Gift. See chapter 3, idea 18. Before going to bed, gather around the tree and share feelings about the day or sing a carol or hymn.

The Week After Christmas

Just because the gifts are open, that doesn't mean that there isn't more fun.

1. Vacation Pals. See chapter 3, ideas 19 and 20.

2. Year-end Sales. See chapter 3, idea 22.

3. Listen. Talk about the Christmas season. Listen to what the family members enjoyed and what you might consider repeating or dropping next year.

4. Thank-you Letters. See chapter 3, idea 21.

5. Thanks to Parents Day. See chapter 3, ideas 56 and 88.

6. Extend Christmas into February. See chapter 3, idea 25.

7. Plan for New Year's Eve. Have a safe family-style New Year's Eve party—perhaps a progressive supper with another family. Each house serves part of the meal and plans a two-generation game. Celebrate for several hours as the new year arrives in London, New York, Chicago, Denver, and Los Angeles. See chapter 3, idea 57 for another party.

❄ ❄ ❄

Depending on the size of your family and the work schedule of parents, you probably won't be able to do all of these things. Be sure that you leave time for "doing nothing," for relaxing with family, walking in the snow, and thinking about the beauty and meaning of the season.

Try some of the ideas that are new to you; ignore others. See if you find some new traditions. The most important activities are those that bring you together with others, that emphasize the art of giving, and that add to your knowledge of the basis for this day—the wondrous life of Jesus.

Make it a merry, meaningful month!

The Best-Ever Christmas

An engraving by Alfred Hunt. From Illustrated London News, *Dec., 1876.*

Chapter Two

The Best-Ever Christmas

A Family Story

There was just one thing Cassie wanted for Christmas that year. The day she saw it in the window at Jacobson's store she knew that this could be the best-ever Christmas in all her seven years.

It was a tea set—plates, cups, and saucers, even a tea pot with cream pitcher and sugar bowl. She'd shown it to her brother, Josh, and even though she knew that six-year-old boys don't care much about such things, he agreed that as tea sets went, it was very special.

The plates were star-shaped with edges of a shiny blue—so bright Cassie thought she could see them sparkle as the family drove by the store one night. The covers for the pot and sugar bowl were topped with a crown-shaped piece also in the glowing blue. She imagined that it would be a perfect set for royalty—and for herself.

One day after school, Cassie made a detour going home so she could see the tea set again. It was just two blocks out of her way, and she'd asked permission. Although there was a mall at the edge of town, the little main street store was still her favorite because its toys were not arranged in stacks by the dozen. Toys at Jacobson's were just not found elsewhere.

There it was, still in the window. She got up her courage and went into the store. Mr. Jacobson was patrolling the aisle where toys were displayed for Christmas buying. She looked up at him and bravely asked if she could see the tea set.

"Only got the one in the window," he said. "When that one sells, that's it. If you want it, you'd better tell Santa Claus about it soon," he added with a wink.

Cassie had known for years that Santa was not the actual giver of gifts, but rather the spirit of love and sharing. So she decided right then that she'd have to plan a campaign to make sure the one tea set became hers.

That weekend, she began the campaign at Aunt Marsha's dinner table. She said, "Do you know what would make the best-ever Christmas for me?"

Aunt Marsha was a librarian at the Rocky Heights Library, and Cassie should have known what she'd say: "Well, I hope you want books—books are the best gift." Cassie looked sad. She did like books, but she liked the tea set more.

She tried the same question on other relatives, but no one seemed interested, and this made her worried that everyone had already finished Christmas shopping. Then, just a week before Christmas, her teenage cousin Andrea stopped over with some cookies. Cassie insisted that Andrea come into her bedroom.

"Look," said Cassie eagerly. "I have everything ready for a tea party. I know the table is a little lopsided; that's because Daddy made it for me, and he's not too good with tools." Andrea looked at the tilted table and gave a bored yawn. But Cassie didn't notice and showed her the tea party guests—her favorite baby doll in one chair, a fashion doll in another, and a woolly tiger in the third chair.

Excitedly Cassie explained: "See, I've even got an apron here because Josh says he'll be the waiter when I get the tea set and have my party. So you see, the tea set is all I need—and it's in the window at Jacobson's." Andrea just shrugged her shoulders and walked out.

The last day of school before Christmas vacation, Cassie made her now-usual after-school detour to look in the window at Jacobson's. But today, right where the tea set had always been was a battery-operated monkey marching around in circles! She ran into the store and found Mr. Jacobson still protecting the toy department.

"The tea set in the window?" he said. "I dunno—I 'spect someone bought it. I can't keep track of everything we sell." Cassie crossed her fingers and hoped her campaign had worked.

On Christmas Eve, Cassie and her family shared a big turkey dinner with cousins, aunts, uncles, and grandparents. Like the other relatives, Grandpa had brought along a shopping bag of gifts to be opened the next morning. Near the top of the bag for her family were two packages about the right size to be a tea set. After everyone had left, she noticed the bag of packages looking somewhat awry. Since Josh was known to be good at peeking, she asked him what he thought of the two suspect packages. "Sure, I felt them all," he admitted. "One is too heavy, but it could be the funny-shaped one on top." Cassie was almost ready to explode with excitement!

Tucked in bed later that night, she thought only of that odd-shaped parcel—would it be the one gift for her best-ever Christmas? When she just couldn't fall asleep, she decided to go downstairs to the kitchen for a drink of water—at least that would be her excuse in case anyone heard her walking down the stairs.

She peeked into the living room where the gifts were now under the tree or placed in the stockings. Daddy had provided big hooks for each stocking to hang from the high mantle over the fireplace. They looked beautiful—and bulging. Dare she go nearer? She thought that just one giant step would be all right. By the glow of the embers in the fireplace, she could see the odd-shaped package sticking out at the very top of her big stocking!

Back in bed she pulled the covers up to her nose and prayed for sleep so that morning could come. Outside her window she watched the snow gently falling—and soon she was asleep.

Then just as the sun began to lighten her room, she was startled awake by Josh's shouting, "Come, everybody. Come and see what happened!"

Racing to the living room, she happily thought, "This is the day of the new tea set!" She was the last to arrive.

Mother and Daddy and Josh were all looking at the stockings. But one—hers—wasn't hanging from the high mantle. Not even the hook was there.

Daddy was shaking his head and saying, "I thought I'd pounded those hooks in so good." Then she looked down on the stone hearth. There lay her stocking, crumpled, packages scattered around it. The odd-shaped package looked as if an elephant had stomped on it.

She gathered the package into her arms and sat on the rug, tenderly removing the tissue paper. There inside was the beautiful blue tea set. But the tea pot had no spout, the cream pitcher had no handle, the sugar bowl had lost its crown, and the plates and cups were in more pieces than she could count. Slowly she looked at each crushed and useless piece.

Then the tears flowed—and flowed some more. Daddy tried to console her by saying he could glue some of the larger pieces together— but they both knew that was impossible. Mother said they could look for another tea set. Even Josh tried to help by offering her a small truck from his own stocking.

A quietness fell over her as she opened her other gifts from under the tree. She tried not to cry as she opened the box containing the new doll who would have sat at the tea table. Books and cars and games were opened, but there was nothing to equal the one lost gift. She certainly wasn't ungrateful, and she didn't want her tears to spoil Christmas for everyone, but somehow she couldn't cheer up.

She lined the box the doll had come in with tissue paper and then began to arrange the broken tea set pieces carefully inside it. Among the pieces she found a tiny card. It read: "I fooled you by pretending I didn't care about your tea set. Have fun with it. Love, Andrea." A little smile came on her face as she thought of cousin Andrea buying this for her, and Andrea's kindness made her feel a tiny bit better.

Josh was watching her put the pieces into the box. "Are we going to have a funeral for the tea set?" he asked. In the past, Josh and Cassie had buried dead bugs and fallen baby birds, and he liked the feeling of comfort it gave him. But she ignored him and took the box to her room, where she put it on her night table so she could see the blue chips as she would fall asleep each night.

Returning to the living room, she said, "This was going to be the best-ever Christmas." Her mother gathered her in her arms and said comfortingly, "Well, it's not even noon yet—we'll have to see what happens later." Cassie didn't think much of that idea. The day seemed hopeless.

But a few minutes later she heard a scratching sound at the front door. "Something's rubbing on the door," said Daddy. "Might be a tree branch blown down in the snow storm. I may have to get my big saw and cut it up." Others in the family looked at each other and hoped he wouldn't find an excuse to use his tools on Christmas day!

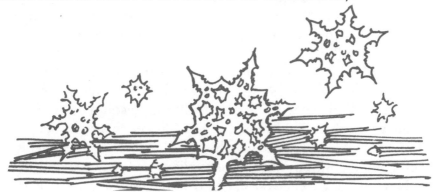

The scratching continued. Cassie was glad for something to do and ran to the door. Through the glass she could see that it was a woolly white snow-covered dog with one black eye and black markings on his legs that looked like boots. He was pawing at the edge of the door—and, in an odd way he seemed to be smiling!

She asked to let it in, and when she opened the door, the dog hesitatingly crept in, cowering with his head near the floor. "Come and see a smiling dog!" she called. They all gathered around to see the bedraggled animal.

"I'll get a towel to dry him off," said Josh.

"I think there are some left-over turkey scraps from last night—he may be hungry," said Mother.

"Okay, I'll fix him a bowl of water," announced Daddy, "but he's not staying."

All the while Cassie and Josh dried him by the fire, the dog still seemed to smile. And when he was offered food and water, the dog put his nose to it and pawed at it, but didn't eat it. This was indeed a strange dog!

As Cassie began stroking his head and nose, the dog jumped abruptly as if in pain, but made no sound. Cassie thought perhaps he'd hurt his face, and she looked at the dog nose-to-nose. "Oh my," she cried, "he's not smiling, his mouth is stuck open!"

Sure enough, he couldn't open or close his mouth! As they looked at the dog, Daddy nudged them all aside, peered into the dog's mouth as best he could, and then announced, "He has one of those small round ham bones caught over the top of his far back tooth. It's like a wedge between his upper and lower jaws. Poor fellow, bring him down to my workshop, and I'll get it right out."

Cassie thought, "Oh, poor fellow, Daddy can't even get a Christmas stocking hook to stay in the mantle—how's he going to get a bone out of your mouth!"

They all trudged down into the basement, and Daddy looked over his selection of pliers, choosing the biggest and fiercest looking one. Josh shrunk back but was told to help lift the dog onto the workbench.

"Now you three hold him still, and I'll get this right out. Cassie, when I say 'now' you try to give his mouth a little push further open." Daddy got in position with the giant pliers. Only the dog smiled.

"Now!" Daddy commanded, and they held the dog and Cassie tried to open his mouth further. Nothing happened because the pliers were too big to get into the dog's mouth.

Daddy next selected a slightly smaller pair of pliers. "This will do it," he said with great assurance, fastening the pliers onto the dog's tooth rather than on the offending ham bone. There was a chorus of "No!" which stopped him from inflicting on the dog unneeded dental work.

Cassie suggested he use the smallest pliers and just get a grip on the bone. "We can give that a try," he said. "I'm glad you're taking an interest in tools."

In a moment, they were all ready for the next try. "Yes, I'm getting a good grip on the bone," he said with new confidence. "Now!" he shouted. Everyone held and tugged, and suddenly the bone popped out.

The dog closed his mouth, then licked his lips. With one giant leap he flew off the workbench and ran upstairs, where he devoured the turkey scraps and took great laps from the water dish. He then went from one person to another—nudging a knee, licking a hand, doing whatever he could to show appreciation.

"We aren't keeping him," Daddy repeated. "We've done a good deed. His owner will look for him, we'll give him back, and that will be that. As we've said before, when you're eight years old, Cassie, we'll consider a dog—a small dog."

This was not a small dog, but Cassie could see it was just the right size for hugging. And, after brushing him, she found that he was a nice-looking dog in a rough-and-tumble way.

Until lunch the dog stayed close by Cassie, and she felt a little happiness creep in. And when they ate, the dog sat a proper distance away from the table and then had a little snooze while she and Josh played a new game. By mid-afternoon, the dog and Cassie seemed to have bonded—two friends who had each had a bad Christmas morning.

In the late afternoon, when the family decided to go for a walk, Josh found a rope and made a collar and leash for the dog.

"If we're going to take him outside, we ought to have a name to call him," said Mother. Cassie was pulling on her snow boots at that moment and quickly answered as if she'd been thinking about it. "Okay, let's call him Boots, since he really looks as if he's wearing black boots."

So they walked through the new-fallen snow, taking turns holding the rope. But Boots didn't seem to need it; without even being told to heel, he stayed right with each of them. "You can see this dog has good manners," said Cassie. "He's handsome and house-broken and obedient."

"Now, don't go falling in love with him," said Mother. "You know he has an owner who's really missing him. He'll probably just stay this one night."

But Cassie noticed that Mother didn't object to Boots curling up at the foot of Cassie's bed that night. And she fell asleep thinking that this might still turn out to be the best-ever Christmas.

In the days that followed, Boots proved to be a truly good dog, playing catch, sitting attentively as Cassie read books to him, and going for walks with all the family.

Daddy used a piece of plywood and some paint to make a sign that listed their phone number and said "Found: woolly black and white dog." He nailed it to a tree at the street corner, smearing the paint so it was slightly unreadable. Cassie hoped it was very unreadable! He also announced that if the owner didn't claim him, the dog would have to go to the Humane Society that weekend. Those words gave Cassie a chill.

It was on a walk the Friday of that weekend that a neighbor commented on the dog. He said he'd seen the dog sitting in a car on Christmas Eve. "I think the car was parked in front of the Rivera house. Why not call them?"

As soon as the walk was over, Daddy called the Riveras. And in an hour there was another telephone call, and soon afterward the doorbell rang. Cassie sat in the living room, stroking Boots. A tall woman entered and said, "Why Byron, you naughty boy!"

This was the owner, Mrs. Drysdale, and she said she had stopped at the Rivera house on Christmas Eve to give them a package. By mistake, the package had been delivered to her house far away on Harvard Avenue East, although it was addressed to the Riveras on Harvard Avenue West.

"How could someone make such a silly mistake of not knowing the difference between Harvard Avenue East and Harvard Avenue West?" Cassie wondered to herself just how special Mrs. Drysdale's neighborhood was. She also wondered why Boots continued to sit with her rather than going over to Mrs. Drysdale.

Next the woman explained that somehow the dog had gotten out of her car while it was parked briefly at the Riveras'. She looked for him as long as she could, but the falling snow and the darkness ended her search. She'd called the Riveras the next day, but they knew nothing about the dog. Who knows where the dog had spent the night, how he'd found the ham bone, and why he chose Cassie's front door the next morning?

In a few minutes, Boots was gone.

Even Daddy seemed to miss him that first night. He went downstairs to the workshop and carefully put away his set of pliers. Somehow, the tools didn't seem interesting anymore.

And that night, for the first time since Christmas day, there was no dog sleeping at the foot of Cassie's bed. She looked at the broken tea set in the dark as tears spilled down her face.

School began again, and at kindergarten all the children were asked to draw a picture of something special that had happened at Christmas. Josh drew a picture of Cassie hugging Boots. The teacher said it was very good and asked if he'd like to take it home to Cassie or put it on the classroom bulletin board. After thinking about it, he decided it would only make Cassie sad, so he tacked it up at the very bottom of the bulletin board where he could easily see it each day.

That week, Mother talked to Cassie about the importance of doing the right thing—how happy Mrs. Drysdale must be to have her dog back—and how we appreciate good things even more when we wait for them. In September, they would look for a nice small dog, she said. She sighed, not sure if Cassie was listening.

Soon no one talked about Boots anymore. Still, Cassie thought about him a lot and wondered if he was happy. The other reminder of

Christmas was the tea set, but Cassie didn't talk about that either. However, the box of broken pieces stayed where she could see it every night. No, it hadn't turned out to be the best-ever Christmas.

Months passed. It was early March, and the snow was getting slushy outside—perfect weather for building a fort in the front yard. One day after school, Josh and Cassie were rolling balls of snow to make a wall when a car drove slowly by. Someone rolled the window down, and both Cassie and Josh instinctively moved back toward the house.

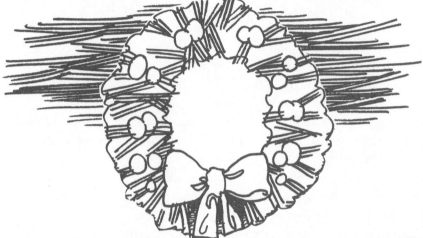

"Little girl!" called a woman's voice from the open car window. The car stopped. Then a woman stepped out—Mrs. Drysdale again! "I've been looking for your house. I tried to reach you through the Riveras, but they must be out of town. It was silly of me not to write down your name and phone number when I picked up Byron."

"Where is he?" asked Cassie excitedly.

Mrs. Drysdale acted as if she didn't hear the question and nervously continued: "You see, we decided to move away—to a warmer climate now that our children are grown. We felt we couldn't keep Byron. No one seemed to want him, and I couldn't remember your name, so I took him to the Humane Society a few days ago. But today I decided to drive over here and look for you."

To Cassie, her words were more painful than the first moment of seeing the broken tea set. She felt anger and sadness and joy and happiness all at the same time. Could this be what Mother meant when she said we are blessed by doing the right thing?

Cassie's words spilled out: "We want him!"

"Yeah," echoed Josh, "We want him!"

Cassie quickly asked exactly where Boots had been taken, and Mrs. Drysdale scribbled the address and phone number of the Humane Society on a scrap of paper. Then, as suddenly as she'd arrived, she drove off.

Racing into the house, Cassie told Mother what had happened. Then she asked if she could phone Daddy at work and see if she could have the dog a little early—"I'll be eight this September," she pleaded.

It seemed hours before her daddy answered. He began, "You know that your mother and I have already talked about a dog." Here was the same answer—Cassie's heart fell. "We agreed you did take good care of Boots—you were very responsible while he stayed with us." He paused, "So let's go and get him!"

The plan was that Daddy would find a way to leave work now and meet them at the Humane Society in thirty minutes. Shortly before closing time, they all rushed in the door and began asking about a dog named Boots. Even when they remembered that the dog would be called Byron, the volunteer at the desk looked confused.

"Why don't you just look at all the dogs. We have many nice ones." Cassie didn't want just any nice dog; she wanted Boots. "Go through that door, and you'll find six rows of cages. It could be that we don't have the one you want anymore, but I'll start looking for his file."

They split up, each one racing down the long aisles, calling "Boots" and "Byron," but no friendly face appeared at the wire gates. Cassie was near tears when a workman repairing a cage suggested she look out in the back exercise area where there were three make-shift cages attached to the supply shed.

Heading toward the cages, she slipped and fell in the mud. It was getting dark. A cold wind blew. Over the P.A. system she could hear the words "Closing time; everyone should exit now." She stumbled along through the slush toward the old shed and the three cages. She wished she had a flashlight.

She looked in the first cage—in a shelter at the back sat a big red setter. In the second cage a small dachshund was curled up asleep, but it opened one eye to look at her. And then there was the end cage—there was no dog at all in cage three.

So that was it—he was gone. Had he been adopted? Was another little girl hugging him at this very moment? Then she remembered what a school friend had told her: Had Boots been put to sleep, a sad but merciful end for an unwanted dog? Her lower lip trembled at that thought.

She gathered her jacket more tightly around her and turned to go and find the others. In the distance she could hear their calls of "Boots" and "Byron" echoing, and then there was silence. The search was over.

Then, for some reason, Cassie looked in the empty cage once more, and as she quietly sobbed "Boots," a woolly heap stirred in a dark far-back corner. At first it moved slowly, then it leaped forward. It was Boots! He pressed his nose against the gate and her hand. He was going home!

Boots became the best-ever dog, and Cassie reminded everyone that it *had* turned out to be the best-ever Christmas. She was heard to quote Mother's words that good things are worth waiting for. Even Daddy fell in love with Boots and promised to build him a dog house, using all his wonderful tools. But he never got around to it, and Cassie was just as happy, since Boots knew that the right place to sleep was on the foot of her bed.

Oh yes, Cassie did get a new tea set for her birthday that September. It didn't matter one bit that it had a green border and pink roses. And she held the tea party with Josh as the waiter. There was home-made lemonade and sugar cookies at each place but one. At that place proudly sat Boots in the chair, a dog biscuit on his plate and a real dog smile on his face.

101 Ways to Make Christmas Memorable

Chapter Three

101 Ways to Make Christmas Memorable

The joys of Christmas are made of little things: simple activities within the family and outreach to those beyond the family. (Outreach is covered in chapter 5, "Sharing the Spirit.")

This chapter gives you 101 enjoyable ideas your family can do together or separately. Some of these take a few minutes; some can be done in the car or at meal time; some will involve several days in December.

These ideas cover eight areas:

1. Christmas Traditions, ideas 1-25
2. Decorating the House, ideas 26-35
3. Trimming the Tree, ideas 36-48
4. Preparing a Celebration, ideas 49-58
5. Making Greeting Cards, ideas 59-65
6. Making and Wrapping Gifts, ideas 66-76
7. Festive Foods, ideas 77-88
8. Symbols of Christmas, ideas 89-101

Don't try to do them all! Choose the ones that best fit your family this year—and save some for another year.

Christmas Traditions

❋ **1. The Christmas Candle.** Place a special Christmas candle on the table and light it at dinner each night in December. If possible, choose a slow-burning candle that is 1" to 3" in diameter. This way, your candle can last for several Christmas seasons.

❋ **2. Storytelling.** Around the first of December, visit the library and look at books about Christmas. (You'll find a list of books, stories, and poems in chapter 9 of this book.) Choose a book like Charles Dickens's *A Christmas Carol* and, each night at dinner, read it aloud for about ten minutes. You'll find that the interest and suspense will increase as the story develops and comes to a climax.

❋ **3. Christmas Angels.** Early in the month, write the names of each family member on pieces of paper and put them in a bowl on the dinner table. Each person gets to pull out the name of another and will be that person's Christmas Angel all month, keeping his or her own identity a secret. Christmas Angels do good deeds for the persons they chose: making her bed, putting a decoration on his dresser, leaving a message under her pillow or a piece of candy in his lunch box. On Christmas Eve, see if each one can guess who her or his Angel was.

❋ **4. Cookie Night.** Select in advance an evening when all the family is available to help. Let each person be a specialist in one kind of cookie—this means that you will have everyone working in the kitchen at one time. It can be wild fun! Show younger children how to roll out dough, cut, and decorate. Store in tight containers or freeze most of the cookies, but periodically bring out a few for munching between Cookie Night and Christmas Day. For recipes, see idea 80.

❄ **5. TV Party.** Look over the TV program guide together and choose a Christmas special everyone will like. Mark the date on the calendar and let each youngster invite a guest. Make popcorn balls in advance or serve popcorn and cider. During commercials, each person moves to a new chair or cushion. Serve Christmas cookies during the last few commercials.

❄ **6. Fabulous Bedtime Stories.** Starting early in the month, make up a Christmas story using the names of the children you're telling it to. Let your imagination run wild. Include things such as toys that talk, a house without a chimney, a reindeer that can't learn to fly straight, a boy who peeks at toys, Christmas cookies that disappear mysteriously, an ugly Christmas tree, and so forth. Tell a little of your made-up-on-the-spot story each night. If you aren't a storyteller, use the stories in this book (chapters 2, 4, 7, and the story "The Search for Christmas," found at the end of chapter 5). When reading these stories, change the names of the characters to the names of your children.

❄ **7. Drive and Spy.** About mid-month, go for a drive to see the decorations in a different neighborhood. Count the Christmas trees already up, and get ideas for decorating the outside of your own home. Sing Christmas carols in the car. Ask a friend or relative if it's okay to stop by. Sing a song on the doorstep. You'll probably be invited in for hot chocolate and a cookie.

❄ **8. Stars in Your Eyes.** On a clear night, bundle up in warm clothes and go outside to look at the stars. In the dark, talk about the star of Bethlehem and the coming of the Christ-child and his message of love. Go around the family circle and ask each to name one thing he remembers about Jesus' life and mission. See how many times you can go around the circle. Sit on a bench, blanket or tarp and count stars.

❄ **9. Big Socks.** Hanging up the Christmas stockings is a well-loved tradition in most homes. Keep up the custom even as kids grow older. Collect small inexpensive items throughout the year. Stocking-sized gifts might include: note paper, a pen, candy, a small wind-up toy, cosmetics, jewelry, a tool. Don't forget a stocking for the pets, too!

❄ **10. The Good Old Days.** Spend an hour with "Christmas Past." Bring out old scrapbooks, photo albums, slides, movies, videos. If grandparents are nearby, invite them to come over and share in these memories.

❄ **11. M&M Night.** Set aside one night as "Mall and Movie Night." Walk through the mall, viewing the decorations, then go to a movie. Or rent a video of one of the classic Christmas movies. Afterward make sundaes of peppermint stick ice cream with fudge sauce.

❄ **12. Amen.** Christmas church services help to emphasize the true meaning of the holiday and bring families together. Even if you haven't been a regular attender, try to go at this season. If your church doesn't have a service on December 24 or 25, visit a Christmas service at another church.

❄ **13. Looking Good on Christmas.** Before bedtime on Christmas Eve, gather the family in the living room while you hide new PJs in each family member's bedroom. (That way no one looks tacky in the Christmas morning photos!) After finding and donning their new PJs, the family members return to the living room for the traditional hanging of stockings. Turn out all the lights in the house,

leaving on just the tree lights. Sit around the tree and talk before bed-time.

※ **14. Can't Wait for Gifts.** Serve Christmas morning breakfast in the living room. Keep it simple. Have Christmas coffee cake and juice and even some Christmas cookies. (See idea 77 for Christmas coffee cake recipes.) No one cares about eggs and cereal on this morning!

※ **15. Hot Fun.** The Christmas potato is a tradition my father invented. He would get up early Christmas morning and bake potatoes, wrap them in foil, and put one in the toe of each stocking. After opening some of the gifts, we found that the pota-toes were still warm and tasted great with a little butter and Parmesan cheese.

※ **16. Slow and Easy.** Gift opening can be done so that each gift and each giver is fully appreciated. Young children are usually anxious to tear everything open quickly, so you need to slow them down. The Christmas stockings can be opened quickly and wildly. Encourage everyone to show what was in each stock-ing. Then, open the other gifts gradually, starting with one per-son's presenting his or her packages to each of the family members. When one person's gifts have been given and opened, go on to the next, and so forth. If you start this tradition when kids are young, you'll emphasize the "giving" part of the day—the savoring of gifts—and it's easier to remember who gave what. If you just turn the children loose with a stack of presents, you'll find that your weeks and months of planning and selecting and your hours of gift-wrapping are over much too quickly. Try out gifts as they are given: let the wind-up toy dog perform; ride the bicycle; take a picture with the new camera. Save one special gift as the last gift to each person.

※ **17. Snow Stroll.** A Christmas afternoon walk (especial-ly after a feast) is a wonderful way to get a little exercise and work off that overfull feeling. If possible, each family member should wear or take on the walk one Christmas gift—a cap, necklace, stuffed animal, and so forth.

❄ **18. Good Night, Dear Book Lover.**   Before bedtime on Christmas night, secretly tuck a book under the pillow of each family member. Books are among the best gifts, and some recipients may start reading that very night. Encourage each one to bring her or his new book to breakfast the next morning and tell what it is about.

❄ **19. Sleep Under a Tree.**   Let the kids sleep in sleeping bags under the Christmas tree the night after Christmas. It's fun to look up through the branches toward the top of the tree, and to fall asleep with the soft glow of the tree lights. For safety, an adult should be sure to turn the lights off after the youngsters are asleep.

❄ **20. Show-offs.**   After Christmas, suggest that children invite their friends to come over and bring along a favorite new toy. If kids are in day-care facilities, arrange for a friend to come home in the afternoon and stay overnight. This makes the last days of vacation-time more fun.

❆ **21. Oh, Those Notes!** Have a traditional "thank-you" letter night and make it pleasant by writing the notes together. Everyone brings note paper and supplies to one room. Play "Stunt" as you write. As they finish each letter, each person is entitled to ask anyone else to do a stunt: somersault, head stand, five push-ups, ten jumping jacks. Small children can draw thank-you pictures, which an older child or parent can letter for them. School children should write one line on the page (not sentences) for each year of their age, with twelve lines as the maximum. Don't correct spelling; it's the thought that counts. How great it feels when these notes are finished!

❆ **22. Next Year's Gifts.** Go as a family to the after-Christmas sales at the shopping centers. See if you can find bargains in wrappings, ornaments, or even find the first gift for next Christmas.

❆ **23. Memories.** Before the kids go back to school, talk about all the Christmas activities that you've done this year. Listen to what the family considers was really fun and worth repeating and listen to comments that would indicate that a particular activity or tradition could be dropped next year. Let kids tell their favorite gifts, too.

❆ **24. More Memories.** Make a scrapbook of the year's events. All year long, have a box into which you toss the kids' noteworthy schoolwork, sports scorecards, programs, birthday cards, travel mementos, your own Christmas card, photos—anything that helps to describe the highlights of the year. Let the kids help paste these in the scrapbook in chronological order. Then, along with help from the kids, write short explanatory notes about the events. Reserve the last page for the signatures of those who helped put the book together. Then look together at "the year that was."

❆ **25. Toy Warehouse.** Let the kids select a few of their new toys, books, and games to put in a box on a top shelf now for bringing out in February. Since most children receive more gifts than they can play with at one time, this keeps some toys for the boring days of winter—and they seem brand-new when the box is brought down.

Decorating the House

❆ **26. The Fresh Look.** Each year, look over your Christmas decorations. You will probably find one that you no longer can use, but is in good condition. Pass it on to a school or thrift shop. Buy just one new decoration each year. If possible, do this as a family or make it a surprise. If it's a surprise, hide it in the house and let the family members look for it, using the "hot-cold" method.

❆ **27. Christmas Everywhere.** Don't put all the decorations in the living room—make the entire house festive: greens on the front door, a bow on your mailbox, a ribbon on the dog's collar. Let kids hang their stockings on their bedroom doors until Christmas Eve. Find a suitable decoration for the kitchen, a bright one for the top of the TV, a small one for the bathroom counter. Decorate mirrors and windows with "snow." If your tree will not show through your front window, consider a wreath with a safe battery-operated or electric candle. Place it so it shows from the street.

Don't forget the outside of your house. Using weather-proof ribbon, decorate your fence or light pole by winding it around like a candy cane. If you have the tools and are handy, cut out plywood figures of the holy family, the three kings, or Santa and his reindeer. Paint them, plant them on the lawn or rooftop, and light them with a spotlight. An always beautiful decoration is a lighted tree. It doesn't have to be a pyramidal evergreen; lights in any tree can be effective.

❆ **28. The Giant's Candle.** An easy and inexpensive decoration is a giant's candle, made of a 5' piece of PVC pipe, about 6" in diameter. Make it into a giant candle by wrapping it with plastic ribbon and wiring a yellow bulb at the top. A peaked piece of plexiglass in front of the bulb will give the light a flame-shape. Plant it firmly in the ground along the walkway to your front door.

❋ **29. Wall of Cards.** Use incoming Christmas cards to decorate an entire wall. Cover the wall from ceiling to floor with a sheet or inexpensive fabric or paper. With straight pins, affix the cards to the paper or cloth in random order (don't line them up too neatly). It makes a wonderful way to enjoy all the art and pictures on the cards you receive.

❋ **30. Artistic Place Mats.** Using white paper place mats, construction paper, or shelf paper, let the kids make place mats for the holiday season. Colored paper, glue, holiday pictures cut from magazines, and marking pens make young designers creative. If everyone makes several, soiled ones can be easily replaced.

❋ **31. One-a-Day.** Children love to open the doors of Advent calendars each day and see the pictures and words inside. Because these are too expensive to throw away after Christmas, carefully shut the little doors and windows when the holiday season is over, and they will be ready to be used again the next year. Tack them up on the kitchen bulletin board or near the breakfast table and take turns opening the window for each day.

❋ **32. Growing Centerpiece.** You can let kids make a green and growing centerpiece for your holiday table. You'll need cotton (not polyester) batting, a dinner plate, a tall fat candle, and about one-quarter cup of sproutable chive or lentil seed (obtained from a health food store). Cover the plate (except the very center and the outer edge) with a layer of cotton. Moisten the cotton, then sprinkle on the seeds. Lightly spray the seeds with water and carefully tip the plate to pour off excess water. Tightly cover the plate with plastic wrap and place it in a sunny place but not in direct sunlight. Uncover to spray with water every other day. Remove the wrap when the seeds sprout. Then rotate the plate and spray lightly with water each day. In ten days to two weeks, you should have a green wreath of sprouts. Place a bright red candle in the center and enjoy your growing wreath on the dining table. However, keep your display in a sunlit place most of the time.

❋ **33. Exchanging Decor.** Choose some of your Christmas decorations that are still good, but not in use. Put your name or initials on the bottom of each one. Ask a few neighbors to do the same. Gather them on a table at one house. For each decoration you bring, you get to trade for another one. It's fun and certainly cheaper than buying new ones.

❋ **34. Stained-glass Window.** At a craft store, purchase green, red, and gold cellophane. Then make your window design out of a large (double) page of newsprint. With a marking pen, draw the outline of a Christmas tree. At the end of each branch, draw a circle. Draw a star at the top and make a mound (like snow) at the bottom. Using the newsprint as your pattern, lay your green cellophane on the paper, cutting it in the shape of the tree. Using narrow transparent tape, add red and gold cellophane balls at the end of each branch and a gold cellophane star on top. Make the mound at the bottom of the tree out of gold cellophane and tape it in place. Now pick up your entire "stained-glass" picture and hold it against a large window as someone else tapes it in place. Depending on light sources, it will look beautiful from both the outside and the inside of your home.

❋ **35. Ho! Ho! Ho!** Put something a little different on your front door. You will need a piece of green felt 48" long and 8" wide, and a piece of red felt 36" long and 12" wide. These are available at craft or fabric stores. Lay the green piece vertically on a flat surface. Using the red felt, cut out 8" tall letters, three of "H" and three of "O," and an 8" tall exclamation point. Leaving some space at the top and bottom, glue one "HO" under another down your banner, and the exclamation point at the bottom. Make red felt fringe for the bottom and a red felt bow for the top. Tack the banner onto your front door and see the smiles it brings to your guests.

Trimming the Tree

❄ **36. Best Bargain.** The purchase of the tree is a good event for the family to do together in mid-December. At the Christmas tree lot let everyone search for "the perfect tree" at "the perfect price." It's fun to give names to trees: The Giant's Tree, The Chubby Tree, The Sad Tree Looking for a Home. Pick one by vote, take it home, and stand it in a cool place in a bucket of water. Celebrate your purchase with bowls of hot soup served with crackers and cheese.

A wonderful alternative is a trip to a tree farm. Here you walk or ride a wagon into the grove, where you select the tree of your choice. In many places you just saw it down yourself; in some places the owners do it for you. Remind the youngsters that the stumps often sprout again and produce more trees.

❄ 37. The Living Tree.

Having a living Christmas tree is getting easier every year because growers are aware of the increasing interest. Now you can find trees up to about 8 feet in height. A tree farm worker can tell you which ones are better for your climate. Choose a tree that is container-grown (as opposed to field-grown and then dug up and put in a container). Ask which varieties are slow growing if you want to bring the tree inside at Christmastime for several years. Your living tree will be happy indoors for about ten days, so plan accordingly. Place it in a bright area but away from heat sources. To spare the tree from heat, consider leaving lights off the tree and decorating only with ornaments. A spotlight will highlight its beauty but should be placed so that it doesn't heat the tree.

❄ 38. Safety First for Your Tree.

There's no time like the holidays to practice fire prevention. Every house needs at least one fire extinguisher to be kept near the Christmas tree, the fireplace, or in the kitchen—the three places holiday fires start most often. Show each family member where it is and how to use it. Have a fire drill to be sure everyone knows how to escape from the house and where to congregate outdoors. Doing this will give you added peace of mind.

❄ 39. No Tipping Permitted.

Some tall Christmas trees sit very precariously in their stands. (Ours tipped forward one year, breaking ornaments, spilling water, and terrifying the dog that was snoozing under it!) Run two thin wires from the top of your tree to a window frame, air duct, or beam. Be sure the wires are high enough not to catch any heads.

❄ 40. Bought at Half Price.

Buy one new ornament for each member of the family during the after-Christmas sales each year (and put them where you'll find them before next Christmas). Wrap these and put one at each place at the dinner table the night the tree will be trimmed.

When youngsters are old enough to move out, let their personal ornaments move out with them, forming the basis of their own decorations.

❄ 41. Designer Ornaments.

Let youngsters—and adults, too—make ornaments out of wood or plastic thread spools, old earrings and other discarded jewelry, shiny paper, colored pipe cleaners, ribbon, Styrofoam shapes, glitter, spray paint, and so forth. If you don't have enough materials already on hand, visit a craft shop for inexpensive supplies and good ideas. Choose one ornament to give to a neighbor or shut-in; let the others be the centerpiece on the dining table until tree-trimming day. Youngsters like to hang their home-made ornaments at their own eye level so they can enjoy their good work.

❄ 42. Unique Ornaments.

Give your tree an international look with ornaments from around the world. There's no need to go around the world to find them, since you can go to shops in your own area that feature foods and other items from different countries. Among the most attractive are the hanging charms from Korea, available at many Korean markets and gift shops. These bright, tasseled ornaments come in many shapes—dolls, drums, vegetables—and cost as little as $2 each.

❄ 43. Clothespins?

Yes, simple wooden clothespins (the kind that have a round head at one end and a split tail at the other end) are the base for some great-looking ornaments. Make them into bugs, birds, and butterflies by first painting the pin or "body." Then, use construction paper for colorful, broad wings, glued on either side of the clothespin. Decorate the wings with sequins or glitter. Small buttons can be glued on to make good eyes.

❄ 44. Lights That Won't Light.

If you unpack the Christmas tree lights a day in advance, your tree decorating day will be more enjoyable. Untangle all those cords of lights and put one youngster in charge of testing and replacing bulbs. An adult can check the cords for worn areas or breaks. These should be very carefully repaired or discarded. Get bulb replacements as needed. Once the tree is trimmed, assign the daily task of checking and replacing bulbs to one person, the daily filling of the tree stand water container to another. You'll be amazed how much water the tree will soak up. It will be more beautiful and last longer if you cut off the bottom few inches of the trunk when first putting it in water.

❄ **45. The Christmas Village.** Some families put a toy train around the base of the tree. Others have small houses set in cotton snow. If you have neither, create—don't buy—your own little village. Find small dolls, cars, trucks, and animal figurines and make cardboard houses. Then personalize your village. Label the dolls with the names of family members. Put your name or favorite store on the cardboard houses. This is truly your little village.

❄ **46. Art Display.** Children make at least one clay piece each year at school. Sometimes it's hard to know what to do with these accumulated masterpieces. Show artists how proud you are of their work by displaying their work under your tree.

❄ **47. Work and Munch.** On the evening you plan to trim the tree, serve supper on the floor around the bare tree. Then go to work. Have dessert as you add the final ornaments and other decorations. Let your dessert be one of the special cakes in the Festive Foods section of this chapter, idea 85.

❄ **48. Packing Up.** When the day comes to take down the tree, let family members write little messages to go in the box with the ornaments and lights. These can be funny sayings, predictions for the year ahead, or other comments. No one gets to look at them until next December. Before closing the box, add some replacement bulbs (bought at a cheap price after Christmas) and some extra ornament hooks. You'll then be ready for next year.

Preparing a Celebration

There are many party ideas in chapter 5, "Sharing the Spirit," that pertain to giving a party for an organization or large group, but here are some that focus on smaller family get-togethers.

❄ **49. Luminarias.** These French paper lanterns, called *lampions*, can be made by youngsters to make your entry say "welcome." (They are traditionally used in Mexico, but they were originally from France, and the idea crossed the ocean with French explorers.) Your youngsters can fold and make their own luminaria bags from sturdy glossy paper or from simple brown paper lunch bags. In either case, fold and make cut-outs in the bag to let light show through. You may glue colored tissue paper inside to diffuse the light and give a stained-glass effect, or you can just leave the bag as it is. For each bag you'll need a glass jar. Put some sand in the bottom of the jar and a votive candle on top of the sand. Carefully light the candles before the guests arrive—and extinguish the candles after they leave. They'll last for many holiday nights.

❄ **50. Surprise.** If you like to entertain during the holidays, consider a Surprise Supper. Each member of the family invites one person to dinner, not telling the others who is coming. The guest could be a business friend, neighbor, school friend, mail carrier, teacher, Scout leader, and so forth. (Spouses of the guest should be included as well.) Thus a family of four will have a supper for eight to twelve. Of course, the person preparing the supper needs to know the total number of guests, but doesn't need to know the guests' names. It's fun to open the front door and see who is there! The variety of guests will make the conversation quite stimulating. After supper, gather in the living room or family room for Christmas cookies. Ask each person to share a favorite Christmas remembrance.

❄ **51. A Wreath-Making Party.** This creative party for teens and adults should take place early in the month so the guests can display the results during the holiday season. Provide a simple buffet supper so the workers can eat as they make their decorations. Big tables set up in a family room or basement work best. Spread a drop cloth or newspapers over the working surface. From a floral supply or craft store, get wire wreath frames for each guest—they'll cost $1 to $2 each, depending on size. You'll need bundles of greens and lightweight wire in sufficient amounts for the size of your group. You will also need a small amount of heavy wire for the wreath hook and rolls of ribbon for the bows.

In the invitation, ask each guest to bring scissors or clippers and small decorations: fake flowers and fruits, small ornaments, glitter spray, dried flowers, tiny toys, and the like.

To make a wreath, first cover the frame with greens, using the wire to hold the greens firmly in place. To cover the wire, pull a few sprigs out from under the wire. Then, affix the decorations and finally add ribbon and a hook.

This is a very conversational party as people eat, work, and comment on others' work. When the wreaths are finished, everyone will be ready to sit down and admire them. One hostess awarded a prize for each wreath: most beautiful, colorful, creative, unique, humorous, festive, flamboyant, and most carefully made.

❄ **52. The Big Feast.** The Christmas dinner is always a favorite event. If possible, rotate it yearly from house to house among relatives and close friends. It's easiest on everyone if it is a potluck event with the host family making the main dish (turkey, ham, beef, salmon) and all others bringing one or two side dishes. Gift grab-bags or wrapped table favors add fun. Let kids set the table, and have those who don't cook do the clean up afterward.

❉ 53. Fewer but Better.

As the extended family grows in numbers, gift buying can get out of hand. At Thanksgiving or some other time when the family is together well before Christmas, have a name exchange. To avoid confusion, agree on an approximate amount of money to spend for a gift. Let all persons put their names and a few gift suggestions on paper. Then, put these in a container and let each one draw one. No telling whose name you drew! This way each person receives one wanted gift, rather than many small miscellaneous ones.

❉ 54. On Your Own.

Many families like to spend Christmas with just their immediate family. But it's fun once in a while to consider inviting non-family friends and neighbors as "proxy" grandparents, cousins, and so forth, to join in your feast. Accept offerings of help so that these guests have a sense of participation just like the family. Ask each person to bring a small gift—$2 limit—for the "Chinese Grab-Bag." This is how it works: Make numbers—as many as those attending—on pieces of paper. Let each person draw a number for the order in which the gifts will be chosen. The person with number one looks over the wrapped packages—no feeling or shaking, just looking—then chooses one, opens it, and places it on the floor in front of him where everyone can see it. Then number two does the same, but may exchange it for number one's gift. And so it goes on. The last person, of course, has the choice of trading for any of the gifts. You then surprise the group by letting number one make one final choice.

If you are going to be without guests, have the traditional Christmas dinner on Christmas Eve so the adults can just relax and have the leftovers to snack on the next day. Share the work by letting younger children set the table, put out serving utensils and dishes, make place cards, seat adults, say grace, and so forth. Teens can make the salad and vegetable. And, of course, everyone helps clean up afterward.

❉ 55. Name Ten.

You'll find some game ideas in chapter 5, but here is one that partygoers of all ages enjoy. It's called "Name Ten." One person is called Master of the Game and makes in advance the necessary lists of ten and also runs the game. Some suggested lists follow, but you can make up your own on any Christmas or winter theme. For example, one list might be of states that get lots of snow. The list would consist of ten states, such as Maine, Connecticut, New

Hampshire, New York, Pennsylvania, Michigan, Minnesota, Montana, Idaho, and Colorado.

The group is divided into two teams. Team one is given the first subject (states with lots of snow) and in one minute must name the states they think have the most snow. Everyone on the team shouts quickly, since they have only one minute to answer. The Master of the Game keeps track of correct guesses and gives one point for each answer that is on the list. Then team two is given thirty seconds to name any remaining ones. They get two points for each correct answer, since it's more difficult. That ends the first round. Then on to the next list, with team two having the first guesses.

Here are some lists to get you started:

1. *Christmas foods:* turkey, eggnog, mince pie, cookies, cranberry sauce, mashed potatoes, peppermint ice cream, cheese balls, candy canes, fruit cake.

2. *Christmas decor:* tree, wreath, mistletoe, crèche, candles, bells, snow, Santa, angels, poinsettia.

3. *Christmas gifts for adults:* ties, jewelry, perfume, appliances, sweater, lingerie, wallet, book, scarf, slippers.

4. *Christmas gifts for kids:* doll, stuffed animal, toy truck/car, bike, book, game, ball/sports equipment, blocks, pet, videos.

5. *Christmas plants:* mistletoe, poinsettia, holly, Christmas rose, pine, fir, spruce, amaryllis, carnation, mum.

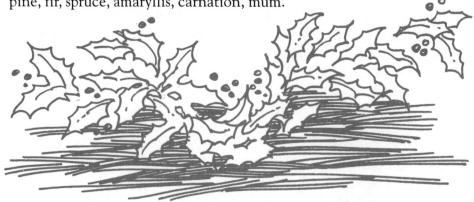

6. *New Year's resolutions:* lose weight, take a trip, change jobs, stay home more, get organized, stop smoking, stop drinking, read a book, get more exercise, live within a budget.

7. *Christmas characters in story and song:* Baby Jesus, Virgin Mary, Joseph, Santa, Frosty, Rudolph, Tiny Tim, Scrooge, Three Kings, Shepherds.

8. *Christmas stories and movies:* birth of Jesus, "A Visit from St. Nicholas" (" 'Twas the Night Before Christmas"), *A Christmas Carol, The Miracle on 34th Street, It's a Wonderful Life, White Christmas,* "Rudolph the Red-Nosed Reindeer," *The Littlest Christmas Tree, The Gift, Holiday Inn.*

9. *Winter outdoor activities:* snowball fight, skiing, sledding, making a snowman, making a fort, caroling, ice skating, tobogganing, shoveling snow, making a snow angel.

10. *Indoor activities at Christmastime:* making cookies, trimming the tree, hanging stockings, exchanging gifts, writing cards, watching TV specials, having a fire in the fireplace, singing carols, attending church, going to parties.

11. *Favorite winter vacation spots:* Park City, Vail, Sun Valley, Snomass, Hawaii, Florida, Mexico, Caribbean, Disneyland, the Holy Land.

12. *Favorite stores/catalogs to get a gift from:* Neiman Marcus, Marshall Field and Co., Nordstrom, Eddie Bauer, Harry and David, F. A. O. Schwartz, Sharper Image, L. L. Bean, Horchow, Victoria's Secret.

13. *Favorite religious Christmas music:* Handel's *Messiah,* "Silent Night," "O Come, All Ye Faithful," "The First Noel," "Away in a Manger," "It Came Upon the Midnight Clear," "O Holy Night," "Joy to the World," "We Three Kings," "I Heard the Bells on Christmas Day."

14. *Favorite non-religious Christmas music:* "White Christmas," "The Christmas Song" (Chestnuts Roasting), "Rudolph, the Red-Nosed Reindeer," "The 12 Days of Christmas," "Frosty the Snowman," "Winter Wonderland," "Jingle Bells," "Deck the Halls," "Here Comes Santa Claus," "We Need a Little Christmas."

You don't need to have a party to play this game—it can be fun around the supper table.

❄ **56. Thank You, Parents!** After Christmas, celebrate "Thanks to Parents Day." Let kids take over the house for a day, assigning tasks, making most decisions, preparing the "Seven-Can Supper" (the recipe is given as idea 88 in this chapter), and finishing the day with activities that they would like to do with their parents.

❄ 57. New Year's Open House.
Change the image of New Year's Day as a day totally devoted to football or a day for recovering from New Year's Eve. Make it a day of friendship and fellowship between the generations. Plan a come-and-go party. Set up one area for the couch potatoes who won't be happy unless there's a TV nearby. Put the food far from them so they have to occasionally get up and walk!

Have a table near the entry door where each person prints in large letters and signs a New Year's resolution. Put these up on door frames, picture frames, walls, and so forth, using easy-to-remove tape. For the kids, ask a teen to be in charge of quiet races. In a quiet race, you don't run, you walk in baby steps (one foot directly in front of the other) so that you don't knock over other guests. (If the weather is good, hold these outside.) A destination is chosen (the piano, the tree, the kitchen door). Each participant is timed baby stepping to the destination and back. The fastest wins a prize, but don't tell that the slowest also gets one.

Trivia games, card games, checkers, board games, and other table games should be available, too.

If you have a VCR, tape the New Year's morning parade and have it showing continuously on the TV screen for those who may have slept through it that morning.

Make food of the assemble-it-yourself variety. Buns with meats and cheeses, tacos with a choice of fillings, salad essentials, coolers full of drinks, and do-it-yourself sundaes (keep a half gallon of ice cream in an ice bucket and refill it as needed).

❄ 58. Twelfth Night Party.
Twelfth Night is the traditional English name for the holy day celebrated January 6. In chapter 6, you'll find references to this celebration, which is held in many countries. It is also called Epiphany, and since the third century it has commemorated the day of Jesus' baptism and the arrival of the wise men. During the time of Queen Elizabeth I, this twelfth night after Christmas was observed with wild celebrations, as in Shakespeare's play of this title. Today, it often marks the end of the holiday season and is a final occasion for revelry. Parties nowadays are usually costume parties for adults as well as for children. Ask guests to come as royalty, members of the court, elves, or

fairies. Food can be simple, but the setting should look regal—connect several tables, use many candles, have music in the background. Give prizes for best costumes. Children's games, such as Hide and Seek and a Scavenger Hunt in the house, are fun for all generations.

Making Greeting Cards

❄ **59. Photo Puzzle Cards.**   Kids love to make these. In advance of Christmas take photos of each child and have large double prints made. Using spray mount adhesive or another good glue, attach each photo to red or green poster board, leaving a border around the photo. For those allergic to glue, cover the photo with clear Contact paper. Leave more border on one side so the children can write their greeting and their names. Then show the children how to carefully use a craft knife (or sharp scissors) to cut the photo into eight to twelve pieces. Place the pieces in a sandwich bag and tie with a red or green ribbon. Address an envelope, slip in the sandwich bag, and mail.

❄ **60. I Chose This for You.**   You'll need last year's Christmas cards for this idea. Make a list of special people and then, looking through the old cards, select one for each person. Cut out the picture, mount it on a folder of colored paper, and write a message on the inside, starting with the words "I chose this picture for you because. . . ." Some "becauses" are that you like to play in the snow, you love the story of Jesus' birth, you'll ride a camel someday, you enjoy the beauty of the winter. These make very personal cards.

❄ **61. Star Cards.**   Most stationery stores carry packages of very large star stickers. Using colored construction paper and photos, kids can make great cards for friends and relatives. For example, paste a picture of Grandma on the front of the card and add a star sticker, placing it partial-

ly over one corner of the picture. Inside, the child writes a short message, such as "You are my star at Christmas and all through the year."

❊ **62. Candle Cards.** Here's another cards-by-kids idea using colored construction paper and a box of colored birthday candles. Cut each piece of 8 x 10 paper in half, and then fold each half in half to form a card. With a small piece of transparent tape, attach a candle to the front of the card. Suggest a short message to write inside each card, such as "Let the light of Christmas fill all your days" or "Put this on your Christmas dessert and think of me."

❊ **63. Out of the Blue.** Surprise someone whom you don't normally send a card to by sending a special card and message. Consider sending a card to your childhood Scout leader, a former school teacher, a childhood friend, the faithful newspaper boy, a neighbor who has moved away—anyone you think of fondly.

❊ **64. Christmas Long Ago.** Grandparents can make very special cards for their grandchildren by sharing what Christmas was like in the old days. Stories of sledding, making popcorn balls, singing in the choir on Christmas Eve, having a tree lit with candles, and other traditions become an enriching part of a child's heritage. Type or carefully write these memories and then glue them onto colored paper folders. Make a different one for each child in the family.

❊ **65. Acrostic Cards.** Youngsters who like to print neatly or have access to a computer can make an acrostic message for a Christmas card:

C	Christmas is a special time.
H	Hear the angels sing to you!
R	Remember Christmas all year long—
I	In everything you say and do.
S	Share love and caring every day.
T	Take time to read the Christmas story.
M	Make others happy; let all strife cease,
A	And blessings will come to you.
S	Soon all the world finds peace.

Making and Wrapping Gifts

❈ **66. Special Wrap.** Make Christmas wrapping paper for special gifts. Use plain white paper, such as shelf paper, sturdy tissue paper, or butcher paper, and poster paints. To make designs, dip washable kitchen tools (such as a potato masher, sponge, whisk, or fork) in paint and "print" on the paper.

❈ **67. Mother's Little Store.** For young children who do not have funds to buy Christmas gifts, create a little "store" where they can shop. Purchase useful but inexpensive gifts for family members—parents, grandparents, brothers, and sisters.

Spread all the gifts on a bed or table in a room that can be private. Invite children into the room (Mother's Little Store) one at a time to do their shopping. (Put out of sight any gifts that would be for them.) Tell them the real price, but give them a greatly discounted price for any gift they want to buy to give to another.

Charge as little as a nickel for a gift to be given by a very young child. (You may have to create opportunities for kids to earn some money.) Raise the prices each year until the kids are launched into shopping with their own money. Provide shoppers with a bag to

carry away their purchases and also supply wrapping materials free of charge!

Mother's Little Store gives children a feeling of participation in gift selection and giving, and it teaches them how to use their money wisely.

❄ **68. Enjoy the View.** Wrap all gifts well in advance of Christmas so that everyone can enjoy how beautiful they look. (An exception would be a gift whose shape is a give-away.) Make it clear that anyone caught peeking into packages loses one package. Work together to wrap gifts for those not "under roof." Play Christmas music on the radio/stereo or ask one family member to read a Christmas story aloud while others wrap.

❄ **69. Clues from Grandparents.** If grandparents (or other relatives) will not be on hand when their gifts to the children are opened, the opening can still be personal and special. The parents hide the gifts in the house and tell the grandparents where they are hidden. Then, at the time they are to be opened, the grandparents telephone the grandchildren and give each one a clue to where it is hidden, such as "It's in the room where parties are held"; "It is just at your eye level"; "It is so high you'll need a short ladder"; "It's where automotive things are kept." This gives the grandparents a sense of participation, and it's also fun for the kids. Youngsters remember "who gave what" more easily when some of the gifts are opened in this special way. Some families set aside the day before Christmas Eve as the day to open packages from special out-of-towners, school friends, or neighbors.

❄ **70. Connecting with Grandparents.** For faraway grandparents, a nice gift is a cassette tape of parents and children talking about their pre-Christmas activities, telling about the school program, tree trimming, perhaps singing carols, and so forth.

If you have the luxury of a video camera, make a holiday video for the grandparents. Show the front door with the wreath, cookies being baked, tree trimming, package wrapping, kids in costume for the holiday pageant, tucking kids in bed, and other activities that grandparents would enjoy seeing.

❋ 71. Cheese Board. From a lumber yard, choose a length of very smooth 1" thick maple at least 8" in width. Have it cut into 8" lengths.

Children can sand the rough edges, then seal the wood with varathane or another sealant. Shop for inexpensive cheese knives or slicers. Tape one to the board, and wrap.

❋ 72. Trivets. Visit a tile company and ask if you can buy a few inexpensive 8" x 8" tiles. Usually they will have odd tiles or old samples. Wash the tiles thoroughly. Next, cut a piece of plywood the same size as the tile. Sand and paint the edges of the wood, then glue it to the bottom of the tile. From a piece of doweling, cut four short legs. Glue these to the wood at each corner. Glue a piece of felt to the bottom of each leg to keep the trivet from scratching the table.

❋ 73. Candle holder sets. Go to a lumber yard and ask for turned posts (those pieces that hold up stairway banisters). Cut these into sections to make sets of three candle holders of different heights. If you are making five sets of three candle holders each, be sure that the turned posts will provide you with the necessary fifteen pieces.

Carefully cut the posts into the desired pieces. Drill the center about three-quarters of an inch deep so a candle will fit in the hole. Sand all rough edges. Then, spray paint one of each set in red, green, and gold. If you wish, you can buy candles to go with the holders and include them with your gift.

❄ **74. Fancy Flavored Vinegars.** During the year, collect interesting tall bottles or buy inexpensive ones. You'll use white wine vinegar as your base, so buy an ample supply, depending on how many bottles you'll fill. In a large sauce pan, put three cups of the vinegar, two tablespoons of honey, and one of the following: a package of frozen raspberries or strawberries, or one quarter cup of shredded citrus peel.

Cover and bring to a boil, then remove from heat and let stand until cool. Next strain out the fruit or peel. Using a funnel, put the vinegar into the bottle, tightly seal, and let stand for at least twenty-four hours. You can now add the strained-out fruit or citrus peel to the bottle if you wish. Cork or seal tightly.

These interesting gifts should keep at room temperature about three months. They can be used on salad greens or on vegetables or as a marinade for meat, fish, or poultry. Put a festive ribbon around the neck of the bottle—you don't need to wrap these any further because they are pretty just as they are.

❄ **75. Napkin Rings.** At a garden supply store, buy a length of PVC pipe with an inside diameter of about 1½". Cut it into sections about 1" wide. Sand the rough edges. Using indelible marking pens, decorate each ring with the recipient's name and/or other designs, depending on how artistic you are. Give them in sets or singly. They make good stocking gifts, too.

❄ **76. New Candles from Old.** Collect all those ugly, stubby candles that you have no use for. Decide on the shapes of your new holiday candles. A cut-off quart milk carton is a good mold for a tall, fat candle. Odd-shaped containers, such as soft-spread margarine dishes, are good for low, flat candles. Tape to the inside bottom of the form a string that can be used as a wick. Temporarily bring it up to the top and tape it over the side.

Next, slowly melt all the candles in a sturdy pan, carefully supervising children during this part of the process. Fish out the old wicks. Add paraffin if you don't have sufficient wax for the candles. Melt in a crayon to change the color of the wax. Cool slightly and then pour into the mold.

After the wax has cooled more, bring the wick string to the center of the wax and tie it around a pencil, laid across the top of the mold. (You can also provide the new wick by inserting a new thin candle at this point.)

When it is totally cool, carefully remove it from the mold. Decorate the exterior with sparkles, and it's ready to be gift-wrapped.

There are many ways of giving. Here is a heart-warming, true story that illustrates one very unique way. It was told to me by a grandmother who lives with her children and grandchildren.

She explained that her finances were extremely limited and that her meager social security check was still being used to pay off debts incurred before her husband's death.

Consequently, she was left with no money for herself or others. She said this didn't usually bother her, since she already had everything that she needed. And she felt she was helping her children by cooking, doing housekeeping, and providing child care. She wasn't a burden; she was an essential part of the family—in fact, her son's wife, Sandra, often said that.

However, not having funds did bother her when birthdays and Christmas came around—times when she wanted to give gifts to her family.

One day, several months after she had moved in with her son and daughter-in-law, she found some money on top of her dresser. She looked to see if the bills might have fallen out of her purse. But no, it wasn't hers. When she asked her son if he knew about the money, he said simply, "It's your allowance. Everyone in this family gets an allowance. Sandra has one for clothes and food; the kids have allowances to cover clothes and social life; I have one for my clothes and lunches. So it's only fair that you have an allowance, too."

He continued, "You taught me when I was little that my allowance was what I got for being part of the family—there were no strings attached. Everyone needs some funds to use—you said it taught self-government and provided dignity. Sandra and I wish it could be more, but this allowance is yours to use as you want. Knowing you, you'll find good uses for it!"

The grandmother protested, but the son was insistent and so she graciously accepted her monthly allowance. That Christmas was the happiest one she could remember in years. She had carefully budgeted her allowance, and along with everyone else, she, too, had gifts to share—thanks to the caring love of her children.

Festive Foods

We associate many special foods with the Christmas season, not just the myriad varieties of cookies, but cakes, punch, appetizers, and foods for family dinners. Here are some that may become traditional in your family. You'll find others in chapter 5, in the section on giving a party for a youth group.

For special recipes from around the world, like plum pudding, see chapter 6.

Consider doubling what you make—it really doesn't take much extra time or work. Then, trade your extras with a friend so you both have more variety in your holiday foods.

❄ 77. Two Great Coffee Cakes. Take your choice or make both.

The Red and Green Coffee Cake

This will look beautiful and taste delicious on Christmas morning.

Ingredients:

¾ cup butter or margarine
1 cup sugar
2 large eggs
2 cups all-purpose flour
2 teaspoons baking powder
⅛ cup candied red citron, cut in small pieces
⅛ cup candied green citron, cut in small pieces

About ¾ pound (1 large or 2 small) Granny Smith or Pippin apples, cored, quartered, and thinly sliced

Almond Toffee Topping (recipe follows)

Method:

In a large bowl, beat butter and sugar until creamy. Add eggs, one at a time, beating until blended. Add flour and baking powder; mix until blended.

Spread batter in a greased 2"-deep, 9" diameter cake pan with removable rim. Place apples on batter, overlapping slightly. Sprinkle with red and green citron. Bake in 350 degree oven until cake top is lightly browned in center and springs back when touched, about 50 minutes.

Just before cake is done, prepare Almond Toffee Topping. Spread hot topping over hot cake and return to oven. Bake until topping is browned, 15 to 20 minutes longer.

Cool in pan about 10 minutes. Cut around pan sides to free topping from pan, and remove rim. Serve warm or cool. If made ahead, cool, cover, and let stand at room temperature until the next day. Cut into wedges. Makes 12 servings.

Almond Toffee Topping:

In a 1 to 1½ quart pan, melt 6 tablespoons butter or margarine over medium heat. Stir in ½ cup sugar and 1 tablespoon all-purpose flour. Stir until blended and bubbly. Stir in 1 cup sliced almonds. Use hot.

The One Pecan Coffee Cake

Ingredients:

2 cups flour
3 teaspoons baking powder
½ teaspoon salt
4 tablespoons melted butter
   or margarine

1 egg
1 pecan
⅔ cup milk
1 can of apple pie filling or
   drained peaches

Topping:

2 tablespoons sugar mixed with 1 teaspoon cinnamon
4 tablespoons melted butter or margarine

Method:

Sift first three ingredients into a bowl. Add the next three ingredients and mix with a large spoon until blended. It will be like soft dough. Using a spoon, spread in two greased and floured round 8" or 9" pans or one rectangular 9" x 13" pan. Don't forget to hide one nut in the dough. (On Christmas morning, the person who finds the nut gets to be the first to give out gifts.) Arrange the fruit on top, pushing it into the dough. Add the topping. Bake at 375 degrees for 30 minutes.

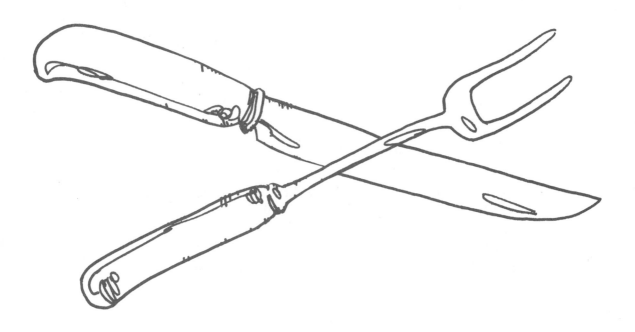

❋ **78. Teaching Carving.** Of course, this has traditionally been the job of Grandpa or Dad, but it's time we teach youngsters—of both sexes—how to carve a turkey, ham, or roast. You'll find instructions with pictures in most cookbooks, and perhaps also enclosed with your turkey. For the first and second time, let kids be "Assistant Carvers," watching the operation and arranging the meat on the platter in an attractive way. You can even have a practice session early in December, using a chicken. When a youngster feels confident, let her do the carving with an adult assisting.

❋ **79. The Turkey Tray.** For our family, who has turkey on Christmas Eve, the turkey tray is the traditional meal on Christmas day. It is made the night before, so it's easy to warm on Christmas day when cooks usually like to relax. After the big Christmas Eve feast, spread leftover stuffing on the bottom of a 9" x 12" pan, then cover with slices of light and dark meat, and spread with sufficient gravy. (I often make extra stuffing just for this purpose.) Cover and

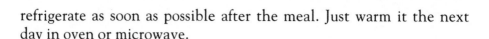

refrigerate as soon as possible after the meal. Just warm it the next day in oven or microwave.

❄ **80. Christmas Cookies.** Here are two great cookies you may not know of.

Peanutty Stars

These cookies keep well—providing the cookie monsters don't find them. They also pack and ship well.

Ingredients:

1 cup firmly packed brown
   sugar
¾ cup peanut butter
½ cup solid shortening
1 egg

1½ cups sifted all-purpose
   flour
1 teaspoon baking soda
½ teaspoon salt

Method:

Preheat oven to 375 degrees. Cream together brown sugar, peanut butter, and shortening. Beat in the egg. Stir together flour, baking soda, and salt and add to creamed mixture. Beat until well mixed. Shape into 1" balls. Place 2" apart on ungreased cookie sheet and flatten each ball. Using a sharp knife, make a simple star pattern on top of each cookie. (To prevent sticking, dip knife in water.) Bake in 375 degree oven for 10 to 12 minutes or until lightly browned. Cool slightly before removing from pan to cooling rack. Makes 4 dozen cookies.

Cream Cheese Brownies

Ingredients:

1 package Duncan Hines
   Deluxe brownie mix
Frosting (recipe follows)

Cream Cheese Filling
   (recipe follows)

Method:

Prepare batter according to directions. Pour ½ of the batter into 11" x 13" pan.

Cream Cheese Filling:

1 8-oz. package cream cheese
2 unbeaten eggs
⅓ cup sugar

½ teaspoon salt
½ teaspoon vanilla
1 6-oz. package chocolate chips

Method:

Beat or blend all ingredients except chocolate chips. Once blended, fold in chips. Spread on top of brownie mixture in baking pan. Pour the other half of brownie mixture on top and spread.

Bake at 350 degrees for 30 minutes or until firm.

Frosting:

2 ounces unsweetened
   chocolate
¼ cup butter or margarine

2 cups confectioner's sugar
¼ cup half-and-half
½ teaspoon vanilla

Method:

Melt chocolate and butter in saucepan over low heat (or in microwave oven). Pour in mixing bowl. Add sugar; beat to crumbly consistency. Add half-and-half and beat with mixer until smooth and creamy. Stir in vanilla. Immediately spread on cooled brownies. Cut into squares when frosting is set. Optional: cover with chopped pecans.

※ **81. Food Wreaths.** For holiday open houses, here are several easy to make buffet items that look like beautiful wreaths.

• Place green grapes, cut in clusters, in a circle on a large tray. Dot with a few cherries and place a big red bow at the top.
• Cut a green honey dew melon into curved wedges and place around the outside of a plate. In the center, place a bowl of dressing made of 1 cup of sour cream mixed with a package of drained frozen raspberries—the red and green combination looks festive.
• Use real Christmas tree greens as a wreath on a plate, with a cheese ball in the center. Make "pockets" of crackers in the wreath.
• Circle a plate with shrimp. Put a bowl of green mayonnaise in the center (just mix ½ cup parsley and ½ cup chopped cilantro into 1½ cups mayonnaise).

※ **82. A Chili Christmas.** A great do-it-yourself buffet can be built around chili. For the base, offer baked potatoes, pasta (such as spaghetti), or hot broccoli. For chili toppings, prepare bowls of grated cheddar cheese, diced avocado, chopped red onions, and sour cream. Use your own chili recipe, canned chili, or try this tasty recipe.

Uncle Milt's Chili

Ingredients:

2 pounds ground beef	1½ teaspoons cinnamon
5 bay leaves	½ teaspoon red pepper
35 whole allspice	2 dashes Worcestershire sauce
4 medium onions, chopped	½ teaspoon cumin
1 clove garlic, minced	1 teaspoon salt
1 teaspoon vinegar	⅛ teaspoon pepper
1 8-oz can tomato sauce	1 quart water
2 tablespoons chili powder	

Method:

Add ground beef to water in 4-quart pot. Stir until beef separates to a fine texture. Boil slowly for one half hour. Add all other ingredients. Stir to blend. Bring to a boil; reduce heat and simmer uncovered for about 3 hours. During the last hour, the pot may be covered after desired consistency is reached. Serves about 8 hungry folks.

Chili should be refrigerated overnight so that fat can be removed from top before reheating.

❄ **83. Vegetables Kids Will Eat.** Try this festive hot vegetable wreath that's easy to make ahead and just microwave at the last minute.

Veggies

Ingredients:

1½ pounds (2 medium bunches) fresh broccoli
1 small head (1 pound cauliflower)
2 medium (about ½ pound) zucchini or crookneck squash
2 to 3 tablespoons butter
2 medium tomatoes
Seasonings to taste

Method:

Trim broccoli and cauliflower; cut into florets all about the same size. Slit the thicker stalks. Arrange on a platter alternately around the outside edge of the dish. Slice zucchini and mound in center.

Melt the butter in a small custard cup (this will take 20 to 25 seconds in microwave oven). Drizzle over vegetables and season to taste.

Cover with plastic wrap, sealing edges well to keep in steam. Cook on full power in microwave 10 to 12 minutes. Microwave ovens vary, so be sure vegetables are cooked until crisp tender. Remove plastic wrap carefully so as not to be burned by steam.

Cut tomatoes into wedges and arrange over other vegetables. Return to oven and cook on full power for one or two minutes to heat through. Makes 8 to 10 servings.

❋ **84. Lovely Lumpy Potatoes.** Folks will learn to like little lumps of green onions in their mashed potatoes—so says Aunt Marie, who shares this recipe.

Lovely Lumpy Potatoes

Ingredients:

6 medium potatoes (cooked
    until soft, then grated—
    a food processor does this quickly)
¼ pound butter

1 can cream of chicken soup
½ pint sour cream
⅓ cup green onions
½ cup grated cheddar cheese

Method:

In a large bowl, stir the butter into the grated potatoes. Then add the remaining ingredients and mix well. Put in glass baking dish and sprinkle with paprika. Bake at 350 degrees for 40 minutes.

❋ **85. Christmas Cakes.** Take your choice of these two great cakes.

Easy Christmas Cake

Ingredients:

Commercial white cake mix

Method:

Follow the directions on a box of white cake mix. Divide the batter into two bowls. Add green food coloring to one bowl, red to the other, and mix well. Bake in two layer pans, and when cool, slice each layer in half and assemble the layers red, green, red, green. Make double frosting so there is enough to go between the layers and on top. Decorate with Christmas candies or sprinkles. The cake can be refrigerated or frozen until needed.

The Christmas Tree Cake

This colorful cake not only looks good, it tastes great.

Ingredients:

⅓ cup margarine or butter softened
½ cup sugar
1 egg
½ cup instant malted milk
   powder
¼ cup milk

2 teaspoons vanilla
1¼ cups all-purpose flour
1 teaspoon baking powder
1 cup malted milk balls,
   coarsely chopped
Frosting (recipe follows)

Method:

Beat margarine or butter and sugar with an electric mixer on medium speed until light and fluffy. Add egg, malted milk powder, milk, and vanilla. Beat for 2 to 3 minutes more or until thoroughly combined. In a small bowl stir together flour and baking powder. With mixer on low speed, gradually add flour mixture to sugar mixture, beating for 2 to 3 minutes or until thoroughly combined. Fold in chopped malted milk balls. Spread into a greased 9" x 12" x 2" baking pan. Bake in a 350 degree oven for 25 to 30 minutes or until a toothpick inserted near the center comes out clean. Cool on a wire rack.

Frosting:

1 8-ounce package cream cheese
¼ cup margarine (half a stick)
¼ cup cocoa
2 cups powdered sugar
1 cup malted milk balls, chopped

1 whole malted milk ball
15-20 M&Ms or similar
   candies
Green prepared frosting in
   a tube

Method:

Cool cake and prepare frosting. In a bowl, combine cream cheese and margarine. Add cocoa and powdered sugar and mix well. Add a little milk to thin frosting if needed. Spread on cake, then use green frosting to draw the outline of a large tree on the cake. Sprinkle the chopped malted milk balls inside the tree outline. Decorate the tree with the whole malted milk ball at the top and the candies on the branch ends like ornaments.

❈ **86. Christmas Crispies.** These make great gifts, party appetizers, or late-night snacks.

Christmas Crispies

Ingredients:

8 oz. sharp cheese, shredded
1 cup margarine (2 sticks)
2 cups flour

¼ teaspoon cayenne pepper
2 cups Rice Krispies cereal

Method:

Using a mixer, cream margarine and cheese. Add flour and pepper. Add cereal. Form into balls and flatten. Press a fork into the top, once in each direction. Bake in a 350 degree oven for 18 to 20 minutes until lightly browned. Cool on a rack. Store tightly covered.

❈ **87. Elf Punch.** Here's a punch you can serve to young and old on festive occasions.

Elf Punch

Ingredients:

8 cups water
3 cups sugar
1 46-ounce can pineapple juice
½ cup lemon juice

1 6-ounce can frozen orange
    juice concentrate
5 ripe bananas
Club soda

Method:

Bring sugar and water to a boil. Cool completely. Add all other ingredients except bananas and club soda. Mash bananas with fork or in blender with some of the liquid. Add bananas to the liquid mixture. Pour into half-gallon milk cartons or a salad ring and freeze. Remove from freezer 2 to 2½ hours before serving. Mix with equal parts club soda (a 2-liter bottle for each carton). Break up into a slushy consistency; therefore, no ice is necessary. Makes more than 20 6-ounce servings.

❄ **88. The Seven-Can Supper.** It may sound strange, but it is a hearty supper on a cold night. All you need is this dish and a salad.

The Seven-Can Supper

Ingredients:

- 1 can chicken soup, undiluted
- 1 can chicken or tuna, drained
- 1 can sliced mushrooms, drained
- 1 can green peas, drained
- 1 can sliced water chestnuts, drained
- 1 cup milk
- 1 can chow mein noodles

Method:

Combine the first five ingredients in pan. Stir together over low heat and gradually add milk. Keep stirring over heat, but don't boil. When ready to serve, remove from heat and add noodles. Stir and serve with a salad.

Symbols of Christmas

The trappings and trimmings of the holidays have deeper meaning if we know their origins. Stories and myths about these symbols abound, and many have now been debunked. For decades the Christmas tree was thought to be a pagan custom, but recently researchers have found a Christian basis for this beloved Christmas symbol.

Make time to share some of these ideas with your family.

❄ **89. The Christmas Tree.** Prior to Christianity, early Romans carried branches to a first-of-the-year celebration as tokens of good luck. The tradition continued, and, much later, Christians from

England saw this celebration and used it as a model for their ceremony of parading with branches at Christmas time.

Long before Jesus, Swedes used branches in pagan celebrations, but with the advent of Christianity, they were the earliest people to include entire evergreen trees in their Christmas celebrations.

A German story—perhaps a myth—originating over 1,000 years ago tells of an English Christian missionary traveling in Germany who finds a group of heathens around an oak tree, preparing to sacrifice a prince. The missionary stops the sacrifice, cuts down the oak tree, and at that spot a fir tree appears. He tells the group that the tree symbolizes Jesus Christ.

❋ **90. Ornaments and Lights.** The Swedish people were probably first to hang objects on their outdoor trees. They used fish nets and tiny painted fish bones. However, when the Germans cut trees and brought them inside, their ornaments included wrapped candies, gold-painted nuts, colorful bird feathers, stars, and angels. Later they added tinsel to the decorations.

When the Swedes began to bring trees indoors, they expanded their decorations to include cookies, apples, and other edibles, which were gradually taken off the tree and eaten.

In Colonial America, ornaments included strings of cranberries and popcorn as well as handmade quilted ornaments.

Today most trees have electric lights, and the ornaments are shiny colored balls. But in the early twentieth century, glass ornaments molded into various shapes became popular. These were in the shapes of animals, Santa, Christmas trees, churches, stars, and so forth. Nowadays storybook character ornaments, ornaments denoting the year, and ornaments that play music or have battery operated parts are popular.

The importance of lights at Christmas comes from Jesus' statement "I am the light of the world." Candles are a symbol of that light. Martin Luther may have been the first person to put lights on a Christmas tree, as a symbol of the stars on the night Jesus was born.

People in Poland were very fond of using many candles on indoor trees—although many families lost their wooden houses due to fires started by the candles.

In Sweden today, a young girl, dressed as Lucia, Queen of Light, wears a crown of candles. In Holland, young men carry lanterns filled with candles as they carol through the towns. In Ireland, a candle is left burning in the window on Christmas Eve to light the way for the baby Jesus.

In the United States, candlelight church services on Christmas Eve are popular. Many carol programs end with the congregation lighting candles and then silently leaving the building, extinguishing the candles when outside.

❋ **91. The Poinsettia.** There is no "point" in poinsettia. This colorful plant is named for J. R. Poinsett, American minister to Mexico, who discovered the plant there in 1828. The plant is common to South America and is a garden shrub in many southern states and California.

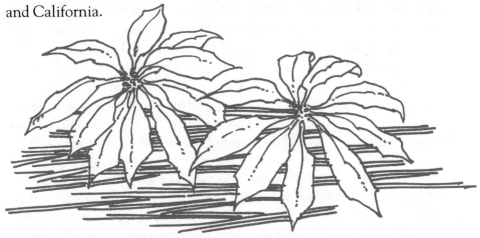

The true flower of the poinsettia is the small yellow center. Special large leaves, called bracts, surround the flower and make a colorful show in red, pink, white, and many special combinations. The contrast of the red with the green leaves makes the poinsettia popular at Christmastime.

✽ **92. The Yule Log.** Fireplaces with large burning logs are a cozy symbol of Christmas. The early Norwegians burned a huge oak log, called Juul, each year to honor Thor, the God of thunder. When they became Christians, they included this tradition in their Christmas celebration.

Other Scandinavian Christians adopted the symbol as well. Then the yule log became popular in England, where an unburned part of the log is used to light the next year's yule log. In Lithuania, the yule log celebration takes an entire evening, and their word for "yule" actually means "Christmas."

In the American South, the yule log celebration was important for the slaves. When the log was lighted, the slaves did not have to return to work until the log burned out. They often poured water on it to keep it from burning too quickly. This was known as "watering the log."

In France, residents of entire towns went into the forests to find and bring home yule logs. On Christmas Eve, a glass of wine was poured over the log before it was ignited. This was followed by a late supper cooked over the fire and eaten after mass.

✽ **93. Plum Pudding.** The story of this traditional pudding comes from the 1500s, when an English king and his hunting party were lost in a blizzard the day before Christmas. All their meager provisions—meat, flour, apples, eggs, ale, brandy, and sugar—were mixed together and tied in a bag, then boiled. The hungry group relished the invention. When they returned home, the recipe was refined, and it became a national dish. You'll find a recipe for plum pudding in the England section of chapter 6, "Around the World for Christmas."

✽ **94. Mistletoe.** More than one thousand years ago, Europeans used this green plant with white berries during their religious gatherings. Because it grows parasitically on trees, it was often a symbol of fellowship.

In pre-Christian times, it was considered a cure for all sickness. It was thought to be so powerful that enemies meeting would lay down their arms when they saw it. It was hung in doorways and corridors as a symbol of harmony between warring factions.

While the origin of its association with Christmas is not known, it is a popular part of American and European customs, where it is hung above door frames. Anyone caught standing under it is supposed to give a kiss to the person catching him or her. However, some say that the person finding someone under the mistletoe has the right to kiss that person. Either way, the custom is enjoyed by everyone but young boys.

❄ **95. Wreaths.** Circles of greens date back to early Christian times as symbols of eternal life. Children wore crowns of greens at Easter in remembrance of Jesus' crown of thorns.

Using wreaths at Christmas was not popular until the early 1800s. Many settlers in America found that evergreens were too precious to cut down for Christmas trees, so they would make a circle of greens for the dining table and adorn it with candles. Today wreaths are generally hung on front doors and are decorated with ribbons, dried flowers and fruit, or small gift packages.

❄ **96. Carols.** Carol singing began in the rural areas of Europe in early Christian times. They were originally happy tunes with dance rhythms, rather than the music of hymns. The word *carol* meant a ring dance accompanied by singing. Religious carols came into being in the fourteenth century as a reaction to all other church music being sung in Latin. Today, every Christian country has favorite carols, the all-time favorite being "Silent Night."

❄ **97. The Star.** This is the earliest of Christmas symbols, being mentioned in the Gospels. It is called the Star of the East, the star that led the wise men to Bethlehem.

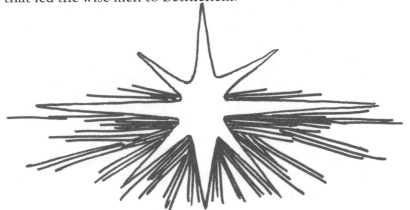

❋ **98. Greeting Cards.** Sending Christmas cards is one of the more recent customs. In 1843 a company in London printed the first card specifically for the Christmas holiday. Twenty years later, another company produced a variety of cards, and these became more popular than the handwritten notes that had been exchanged up to that time.

In America, a Boston lithographer marketed cards to Europe in 1865. It wasn't until ten years later that they were sold in the United States. Today most everyone sends cards—individuals, businesses, dentists, milkmen. Cards in newsletter style that chronicle the year's events have become common in the last few decades despite many humorous remarks about them.

❋ **99. Saint Nicholas and Santa Claus.** There was a real person by this name who was bishop of Myra in Asia Minor in the third century. He was a good and generous man and had the practice of giving surprise gifts to other worthy people. Soon all surprise gifts were credited to him.

In Norway there was a tradition that gifts were brought by a character who entered the house via the chimney. In the Netherlands, there was a St. Nicholas, who was the patron saint of children. His fame traveled throughout Europe, and his name was translated into many languages. He is called Père Noel in France. In Switzerland he is called Christkindli. And in Italy it is a female character, La Befana. For children around the world, he is the most favorite symbol of Christmas.

From these earlier European characters comes the American Santa Claus symbol, which combines many myths. Dutch settlers in New York called St. Nicholas Sinterklaas, and from that the American name Santa Claus developed. Then, in 1823, a minister named Clement Moore wrote about this character in a poem entitled "A Visit from St. Nicholas"—more commonly called " 'Twas the Night Before Christmas." It was here that the reindeer and sleigh, the jolly appearance of the character, and the filling of stockings came into being.

The myth of a Santa Claus continues today, and while many children firmly believe it, some parents choose to teach their children that Santa Claus is not a real person but rather the spirit of love and giving that we cherish at this season.

❄ **100. Stockings.** The hanging of Christmas stockings stems from the Moore poem. However, hundreds of years before in Europe, leather boots were used for gift receptacles. In Holland, wooden shoes were placed where St. Nicholas could find them, and they were filled with straw for St. Nicholas's horses or deer. For good children, the straw was removed and replaced with toys. For bad children, the straw was removed and replaced with a stick—to be used to beat the child into goodness.

Today, oversized stockings are "hung with care" by both children and adults.

❄ **101. The Manger Scene.** This is also called a crèche, a crib, a nativity set, or a cradle scene.

People throughout time have tried to bring Christ back into Christmas. One was St. Francis of Assisi. He did not like the sermonizing at Christmas or the manger scenes lavish with silver, gold, and precious stones. To him, they seemed far removed from the little cave in Bethlehem, and also far from the simple people. So in a wooded area, he made a life-sized manger with hay, thatch, and plain wooden figures, and a live ox and ass were led in. It was so popular that an English visitor took the idea with him throughout Europe.

Thus began the tradition of building simple "Bethlehems" outdoors, in churches, and most of all in homes. Clay figures were used and reused for generations. Soon, smaller, tabletop versions became popular.

In Europe, the manger scene is the main Christmas decoration, and children light the crèche with candles and sing carols around it before going to bed.

Brian and "The Bing Bong Carol Song"

"*Winter Sports—Coasting in the Country,*" by Granville Perkins.
From Harper's Weekly, *Feb. 17, 1877.*

Chapter Four

Brian and "The Bing Bong Carol Song"

A Story About Gradeschoolers

Everyone will have a part in the school's Christmas Pageant!" That's what the announcement said, and Brian excitedly carried it home from school. It was early December, and the program would be on the evening of the last day of school before the holiday vacation. He put the paper in the middle of the dinner table and said: "The sixth graders get the big parts. We get to choose what we want to be, unless someone else signs up for the part first. That's what Miss Dombrowski says, and she's in charge. So I'm going to get to school early tomorrow morning so I can have the part I want."

Brian's mom, who worked as the fabric buyer for the discount warehouse, sighed and said, "And I suppose I have the honor of making your costume." She smiled and added, "But that's okay; at least I'll be able to buy the material at a good price."

Holly, one of Brian's sisters, piped up, "Be the baby, Brian. Then you don't have to learn any lines, except 'Wah, wah.'" His other sister, Polly, giggled.

Holly and Polly were eight-year-old twins, and Brian always thought they had weird ideas. After all, he was almost thirteen and the man of the family since Pops had left a year ago. The twins didn't understand this sudden change in the family—no Pops on the scene. And they especially didn't understand how very hard it was on Mom to work long hours and keep the family together.

Polly, not wanting to be left out of the conversation, said, "Yes, volunteer to be the baby, and Holly and I will make swaddling clothes for you to wear."

"Very funny," said Brian, "but I don't want to be baby Jesus. Besides, the part is taken. That art teacher, Mrs. Krebs, is loaning her new baby to be the baby Jesus in the pageant."

Mom smiled, "How sweet—a real baby on stage. Then what part do you want to play? There really aren't that many leading roles, you know."

Brian looked thoughtful. "Everyone at school is going to be in the show. Some will be in the chorus; others will give out the programs; little kids like the twins will be angels. The older kids have the choice of being on the stage crew or having a speaking part. I've decided I want to play the part of Joseph."

The next morning, Brian raced into his classroom. Miss Dombrowski had put a list of all the parts on the blackboard. Girls who didn't want to learn lines were signing up as singers, since they already knew most of the carol words. Many of the guys were on the stage crew, but Amanda Shipstein and Maria Gonsalves—two girls that Brian liked—had signed up for the stage crew, too. He hesitated a moment. Should he join the stage crew? No, he would sign up to be Joseph.

Chalk in hand, he looked at the list of characters. Opposite the word Joseph was written the name of Rob Hunter. *Rats*, Brian thought, *he beat me to it*.

Miss Dombrowski noticed Brian frowning at the list and said, "If two people want the same part, we'll just draw straws." So Brian wrote his name after Rob's.

At recess, Rob gave Brian a friendly poke and said, "Hi, Joseph." Brian did the same thing in return.

Then Rob said, "Did you know that Annie McLaughlin is going to be Mary? I wonder if Joseph gets to kiss her? I sure wouldn't mind that."

After recess, Brian erased his name from the blackboard. Yes, Rob could do that mushy stuff, but he definitely wasn't going to kiss a girl in front of the whole school and all those parents!

That night at supper Mom asked if he'd gotten the part of Joseph so she could get some brown burlap material and start on his costume.

When Brian told what had happened, Holly said, "Boy, did Rob ever fool you. There isn't kissing in a Christmas pageant!"

Polly added, "By drawing straws, Rob had only a 50 percent chance of getting the part. But with a few silly words to you, he had a 100 percent chance."

When Brian hung his head, Mom said, "Now, just go early tomorrow morning and look at the list. I'm sure there's still a good part left for you."

And there was! Brian noticed that no one had signed up as Head Shepherd. So he quickly put his name opposite that part.

Rob Hunter watched him writing and then said, "Come over here, Brian, I'm going to clue you in on something. Coach Yamada coaches, but he also has a little farm, right?"

Brian agreed. Everyone at school knew that.

"And," Rob continued with a gleam in his eye, "he is going to let the school borrow one of his lambs for the pageant. In fact, the Head Shepherd will get to carry it."

"Way to go!" said Brian. He'd never even seen a live lamb—much less held one. "That will be great!"

"Not so great," countered Rob. "You know why no one has signed up for Head Shepherd?"

Brian shook his head.

"Because," and here Rob spoke slowly, "we all know that little lambies are very excitable. Pick him up, and he'll poop right in your arms—right in front of everybody!" Rob walked away, his head thrown back with laughter.

It wasn't until after school that Brian could erase his name from the part of Head Shepherd. He anxiously glanced down the list and noticed that no one had signed up for King Number Three.

So at dinner that night he was ready for the usual questions about the school program. He proudly announced that he was going to be King Number Three.

Mom smiled. "I just knew I wouldn't get away with making you a simple costume. Now, I get to make you an elaborate robe and a crown." She gave his arm a loving squeeze. She knew how hard it was for him without Pops at home—even though in the past her husband had usually been too busy to show much interest in the kids.

The twins said almost in unison, "Mom will make you look great." And Holly added, "You always act like a stuck-up king anyway."

And so at the end of the day on Friday, all the parts had been selected, each class had at least one song to learn, and the entire cast had to memorize all the verses of "I Heard the Bells on Christmas Day" for the big finale.

Kindergarten and grade one kids were going to be behind a special scrim curtain, singing "Away in a Manger." Fourth and fifth graders were to be shepherds and also sing. And, of course, the sixth graders would have the speaking parts and important things to do on the stage crew.

Grades two and three—and that included Holly and Polly—were to be angels and sing angel songs. The big news was that Coach Yamada was going to wire one angel so he or she could actually fly across the stage. This sure wasn't going to be an ordinary pageant!

The next day the twins came home from school with samples of the white gauze material for their costumes and the silver tinsel for the halos and the trim on their wings. Mom said it wasn't much harder to make two of the same costume if the twins would just stand still while she measured them.

As she draped the material around them, Brian couldn't resist saying, "Well, this is as near as you two will ever get to being angels."

On the next Monday, the kids brought another notice home from school, one asking all fathers to volunteer a few nights to help build the sets. This was going to be a really big production! There would be one scene on a roadway with the skyline of Bethlehem in the distance, another scene in a field, another in Herod's palace, and the final scene in the stable.

After Mom had read it, Brian rolled the notice into a ball and threw it in the trash. Certainly his Pops wasn't going to help build the sets. He wasn't going to help on anything.

It had been just before Christmas last year that Pops had moved out. He had said that it would be just for "a little while," until he got his work better organized. "A little while"—what a joke. After a few months he heard Pops tell Mom that it was too hard on him to have a stressful job and at the same time cope with three kids when he got home. So he now lived in another part of the city and didn't even come to see them unless Mom called him up to remind him.

Yes, his parents were definitely separated, but Brian also felt very much separated.

Mom sensed his sadness. "It's okay, Brian. Our family is doing its part for the pageant, even though Pops isn't helping build scenery. I called Miss Dombrowski today and volunteered to be costume coordinator. The store says I can take all that I need of the fabrics that aren't selling well."

So in a week the pageant was well under way. In the music class, Mr. Schernholz rehearsed groups of singers as well as the soloists. One afternoon he asked the three kings to come forward to try their song.

"I have to sing?" blurted out Brian.

"Of course," said Mr. Schernholz, "didn't you know that? Your song is 'We Three Kings,' and as King Number Three you get to sing the third verse."

"You get the yucky words," taunted King Number One proudly.

Mr. Schernholz handed out the music, and Brian gloomily read his lines:

> Myrrh is mine; its bitter perfume
> Breathes a life of gathering gloom;
> Sorrowing, sighing, bleeding, dying,
> Sealed in the stone-cold tomb.

"Wow, those are heavy words," Brian complained.

Mr. Schernholz cut in. "Don't worry about the words. Miss Dombrowski says she's going to change them a bit for you. So just work on the tune this weekend."

Saturday afternoon, Brian brought the song to Mom and asked, "How does this tune go? I only know the part that goes 'O star of wonder,' but this part I don't know at all."

Mom sat down at the old piano and picked out the melody, and they sang together for a while. By Monday morning, Brian could sing it perfectly. *This wasn't going to be so bad after all*, he thought. Amanda and Maria on the stage crew would get to see him as a king, and that wouldn't hurt their impression of him at all.

That afternoon, Miss Dombrowski gave him the revised words, which he liked much better. All that week he practiced:

> Myrrh is mine; the gift that I bring.
> Prophecy is what I must sing.
> Praying, preaching, healing, teaching,
> That is our newborn king.

By the middle of the week, Mom had created three beautiful brocade robes. One was in bright blue with gold trim. One was black with silver trim. And the one for Brian was ruby red with green trim. Each king had a different crown, and Brian's had big shiny fake jewels set into it.

Miss Dombrowski was thrilled with their elegant appearance as the boys tried on the robes. Then Mr. Schernholz asked the kings to sing

their song for the class. Amanda was in charge of props, and she carefully brought each king his crown. When she got to Brian, she placed it on his head and patted his hair into place. *Yes*, thought Brian, *I was meant to be a king!*

So the song began. The first king sang out clearly in a boyish soprano voice. Next, the second king sang his lines perfectly. Then it was Brian's turn.

"Myrrh is mine" came out just fine. Then something totally unexpected happened as he sang the line "the gift that I bring." His voice cracked and went out of control, up and down like a crazy yo-yo.

While the class giggled, Miss Dombrowski rapped for attention and quietly asked Brian to start again. Mr. Schernholz played the lead in, and Brian sang, "Myrrh is. . . . " And that was as far as he got when his voice cracked again.

"Do you have a cold?" Mr. Schernholz asked.

"No, sir," Brian replied in a whisper, looking down at his shoes.

"Well, it may be that your voice is changing. But that usually doesn't happen quite this soon."

But that was what it was. In fact, the next day it was worse. Brian just couldn't sing anything on the right notes, and he felt like giving up talking. His hands stroked the fabric of his robe, and he realized that Amanda would never put the elegant crown on his head again. He would have to be replaced as King Number Three.

That night his mom tried to console him. "Well, your voice's changing means you're growing up. Soon you'll have a nice deep voice like your Pops."

Double hurt, thought Brian. He'd already sent a flyer about the pageant to his Pops—and on it he'd added a note about the wonderful robe Mom had made and how he was playing the part of a king. Now someone else would get to wear that robe.

The next day that someone else was chosen. It was his good friend, Perry Peterson. They were the same size, and Perry's voice was high, clear—and steady.

It was decided that Brian and Perry would just change jobs. Perry had been in charge of special effects. That meant the star and the big bell.

"It's a piece of cake," Perry said. "The dads have made this star of shiny mylar, and they've wired a light inside so it glows. It's on a long black pole. All you have to do is climb a ladder, and at the right time you lower the star out and over the group of shepherds as they sing 'The First Noel.' You slowly lower the star during the second verse when the words say:

'They looked up and saw a star
Shining in the east, beyond them far;
And to the earth it gave great light,
And so it continued both day and night.' "

And Perry continued, "This is really a fun job, because, like I said, you climb this moby ladder and let the star down so everyone can see it. Your only other job is to ring the big bell at the end of the pageant. You have to make it go bing and bong at just the right times during the song." Brian nodded, and Perry continued, "The song's real title is 'I Heard the Bells on Christmas Day,' but everybody on the stage crew calls it 'The Bing Bong Carol Song.' "

So once more Brian had a new job in the pageant. He had wanted to be Joseph, but he was tricked out of that role. Then he was going to be the Head Shepherd, but he decided against holding a real live lamb. Next he was King Number Three, except he couldn't sing. Now he was in charge of a star and a bell.

That afternoon on the way home from school he told the twins. He thought they'd make fun of him, but instead they were impressed, and Holly said, "Have you seen that ladder? It is soooooo tall. It has to be that way to reach above the olive trees and tall palm trees in the shepherds' scene."

That afternoon, Pops called. Brian explained about his switching parts from Joseph to Head Shepherd to King Number Three to the person in charge of the star and the bell.

"Okay, I'll be there because I want to see the twins as angels, and I want to see you in your new important role. Besides, I miss you. Let me talk to Mom; I want her to know I'll be there, too." Brian tried to listen as his parents talked. How come they couldn't all live together in peace?

When the phone call was over, he asked his mom once more why Pops had left. She tried to put it in words that had meaning for Brian.

"It isn't that he doesn't love us. He just couldn't handle all of the problems of work and family life. Traveling five days a week, trying to be with us weekends, he never had any time for himself, never had any quiet time to think. Then, as things got busier and busier before Christmas, he just felt he was falling apart, so he moved into that little apartment until we could sort it all out."

Brian argued, "But it's been a year! That was a bad Christmas without Pops, and you've had to do everything all year. Now we're coming to another Christmas without him. It's not fair to us, and it's not fair to you, either." Brian's anger showed.

"But you three are a big help to me," she responded.

"I want to be a regular family," Brian shouted.

Quietly, his mom said, "We *are* a regular family. There are lots of families nowadays with one parent, and they do just fine."

"But we all still love each other—I know you love him, and we miss him . . . and love him, too."

"Maybe we can talk about it when he comes home for the pageant."

Finally, it was the week of the pageant. Friday was the big night, and the dress rehearsal was scheduled for Thursday afternoon. Each class now knew the words to its carols. The programs were printed. The costumes were finished. The sets and props were all stacked in the wings of the stage in the gym.

Brian had to agree that Holly and Polly looked great in their angel outfits, wings flapping and halos just a little crooked. When they had all gathered in the gym, Coach Yamada announced that the school board had axed the idea of a flying angel. Although the angel would have had a harness and two ropes, they thought it was just too dangerous to be flying over the stage. So all angels would stand on risers instead. Holly and Polly and all the other angels grumbled. Each had hoped to be the flying angel. And now there would be no flying angel.

But it was time for the dress rehearsal to begin. The first scene was on the road to Bethlehem. The dads had made a large plywood donkey with wheels behind the four feet. Mary was to ride on it as Joseph pulled it across the stage. It rolled along effortlessly until it hit a bump in the old floor. Annie McLaughlin, who had been looking serene as Mary, suddenly went flying off the donkey onto the floor. She giggled when she got up and quickly said she wasn't hurt, but added that this was no way to treat a woman who was going to have a baby. Everyone laughed.

Miss Dombrowski then said something that captured the entire school's attention. She said that it was an old theatrical tradition that when things went bad during dress rehearsal that was fine, because it meant things would go well at the actual performance.

Well, they all hoped that was true because from that point on, everything began to go wrong. The live lamb did just what Rob had prophesied.

Coach said, "Good, he's got that out of his system," as he winked at Miss Dombrowski. "Yes, let's be happy that everything is going wrong at the rehearsal so it can go right at the performance tomorrow night."

Next it was time for the shepherds' scene. They gathered among trees in front of the starry backdrop. Brian took the star with its long heavy pole and trailing electric wire. The extension ladder was put in place in the center behind the scenery. Carefully, step by step, he climbed up into the darkness above the stage. He waited at the top, looking down at the scene below. Around him hung various ropes like spaghetti—leftovers from the aborted flying angel gimmick.

The shepherds sang the end of the first verse: "Noel, Noel, Noel, Noel, born is the King of Israel." That was his cue. The next line would be "They looked up and saw a star. . . . " The faces of the shepherds turned upward toward him on his perch.

He extended the pole. The star dangled from it on an invisible cord. Someone in the wings turned on the switch. The star glowed. Brian slowly lowered it into view.

The shepherds continued, "And to the earth, it gave great light." Brian felt thrilled as the lighted star gave a special glow to all those

below. As the curtain closed at the end of the carol, Brian hauled the star upward and then proceeded to back down the long ladder to the floor.

He jumped the last few steps since he saw Maria Gonsalves standing nearby, holding one of the fake furry lambs. "The star was wonderful!" she said. And Brian felt that the word *wonderful* was as much for him as for the star.

Just as Brian was thinking what to say next, Rob Hunter walked up with Amanda. She said, "Wasn't that star just perfect, Rob?"

Rob gave a flirty smile to Amanda and said knowingly, "Yes, but you know what they say about dress rehearsals. You really want things to go wrong, so they'll go right when it really counts at tomorrow's performance." And looking at Brian he added, "Better be extra careful on that ladder tomorrow night, old buddy."

There was no time for Brian to think about Rob's stupid remark. The scene in the stable was now set up, and Rob and Annie and a doll substituting for the real baby were getting into place. Brian put the star in a safe place and went to find the big bell he was to strike for the finale.

Amanda and Maria followed after him. Amanda said, "We're having a Christmas party for the sixth grade cast and crew on Saturday. Want to come?"

Brian felt he wanted to say yes, but he knew his Pops would still be at home. So he asked if he could let them know early Saturday morning when he knew Pops's plans. The girls looked a bit disappointed but agreed. *Why do two good things happen at the same time?* he wondered.

The stable scene was the most complicated one in the pageant. The innkeeper tripped on his robe, but everyone thought that was funny. Besides, he wouldn't do that Friday night.

The shepherds walked noisily into the scene, their shoes and staffs making thudding sounds on the wood floor. Miss Dombrowski made them exit and enter again. "Walk with reverence and awe," she said.

The angels lined up on their risers, and one fell off, losing both her halo and her wings.

The first graders behind the scrim curtain looked like baby angels as they sang "Away in a Manger" until one accidentally shoved another and the song soon became a pushing match.

As the kings made their grand entrance, all three crowns fell off and rolled to the edge of the stage and then into the audience area. Amanda made a note to bring some hair pins to hold them in place.

A team of fourth graders was putting up hundreds of folding chairs and making such a racket that Joseph and Mary soon were shouting at each other.

Everyone seemed pleased with the day's mistakes and joked how really perfect the performance would be the next night.

Finally came the grand ending. Everyone gathered around the sides of the stable to sing "I Heard the Bells on Christmas Day." This was Brian's big moment. He had to make sure that he rang the big farm bell at just the right times. And it was only to go "bing bong" and then be silent again.

Miss Dombrowski had told him how the bell in the tower of the Church of the Nativity rings each year just at midnight as Christmas Day begins. And she told him how radio stations around the world record this glad tolling of the bell. So he figured he'd better do it perfectly.

Everyone joined the singing: "I heard the bells on Christmas Day, their old familiar carols play."

Bing bong went Brian's bell.

"And wild and sweet the words repeat of peace on earth, goodwill to men."

Bing bong went the bell again.

"I thought how, as the day had come, the belfries of all Christendom. . . ."

Bing bong perfectly again.

" . . . Had rolled along th'unbroken song of peace on earth, good-will to men."

Another perfect bing bong!

"And in despair I bowed my head. 'There is no peace on earth,' I said."

By now all the stage crew had gathered around Brian to watch him control the big bell as it bing bonged again.

" 'For hate is strong, and mocks the song of peace on earth, good-will to men.' "

Yes, another flawless bing bong!

And then came the last verse: "Then pealed the bells more loud and deep: 'God is not dead, nor doth He sleep.' "

Bing bong more softly this time.

" 'The wrong shall fail, the right prevail, with peace on earth, good-will to men.' "

And then came Brian's personal triumph of bell ringing—one big bong after another as the stage crew applauded and the curtain closed.

"It was beautiful," said Amanda. "You should take up bell ringing as a profession."

"You got it all so right each time," said Maria, touching his arm. "I hope you can do it just that way tomorrow night."

Even Miss Dombrowski said it was perfect, and Coach Yamada slapped him on the back.

Only Rob said, "Yeah, perfect today. Just watch out for tomorrow night! It will probably be bong bing bung."

That evening, Brian helped the twins make the kind of Christmas cookies that Pops liked. And they noticed that their mom had the house decorated with a bright new poinsettia plant, the traditional manger scene, a wreath on the door, and the space cleared for the Christmas tree they were going to decorate that weekend. As she hugged them each before bed, she said, "Tomorrow is going to be a big day for all of us." Brian hoped that her bright smile was for both the pageant and for Pops.

Would he come? wondered Brian. Or would the thought of family and Christmas in addition to work again be too much for Pops? Brian fell asleep hearing the sweet bing bong of the bell echo in his memory.

After school the next day, Brian and the twins hurried home to get ready for Pops's arrival. But when they got near the house, they recognized Pops's car already in the driveway. He greeted them with hugs at the door, and they couldn't help noticing a pile of Christmas presents in the living room.

"Will you stay and help trim the tree this weekend?" asked Holly.

"Will you stay and have Christmas with us, please?" begged Polly.

Brian was quiet and searched his father's face for some answer.

"Wait a minute," said Pops. "I said I'd be here to see you in the pageant, and I'm here. Mom called from work to say she'd like all three of you to take a little nap so you'll be rested for tonight." The twins groaned, but when Pops scooped up one under each arm, they willingly went to stretch out on their beds and soon fell asleep.

Down in the living room, Brian was sprawled on the sofa. Pops sat on the floor next to him.

"How's it going, Sport?" Pops asked.

"Okay," said Brian, "but we miss you."

"Well, I'm working on that. I may get a transfer to the main office here, but I'm not sure how I'll like it. At least I could be home more during the week."

"That would be great, and Mom would like it, too," said Brian.

"Your mom is a good woman. She's doing a fine job with you. I can't wait to see you in the show tonight."

"It's going to be good because it was so bad yesterday," said Brian.

"What do you mean?" asked Pops.

So Brian explained to him about the theatrical tradition that bad dress rehearsals mean good performances. Pops laughed and asked if everything went wrong at the dress rehearsal.

"No," said Brian, "the way I hung the lighted star from the big ladder was just perfect. And the way I rang this huge bell in 'The Bing Bong Carol Song' was perfect, too."

"But you're certainly not thinking that just because you did it right at the rehearsal you'll mess up tonight, are you?" asked Pops.

"Well . . . " said Brian slowly, "some of the guys did warn me that I might really spoil the show tonight."

"That's just humbug," said Pops and put an arm around Brian. "You just rest up. I want to surprise your mom by having supper ready."

It was just like the old days—all of them sitting around the table eating and talking and laughing. Soon it was time for the twins to be helped into their angel costumes and all of them to leave. Brian loved sitting between Pops and Mom in the front seat as the winged angels hovered in the back seat. *A real family*, he thought.

When they arrived, Mom went to check that all the costumes were perfect before she joined Pops in the audience.

The pageant began with Miss Dombrowski making a little speech of welcome. Then, the curtains opened.

The wooden donkey rolled perfectly across the stage, and Annie McLaughlin didn't fall on the floor. And no one tripped on the long robes. The kings had their scene with Herod, and their crowns stayed on their heads, pinned tightly in place. Everything that went wrong the day before was going right tonight.

Brian noticed that Coach Yamada had put a diaper on the live lamb tied backstage. He whipped it off as the shepherds' scene was to begin. The fake furry lambs were put in place under the trees, and the Head Shepherd picked up the live lamb and walked to the center of the stage.

Brian began his climb up the long ladder, carefully holding the star on its pole. He threaded his way among the ropes that hung down from the ceiling. In place, he found that if he leaned a little forward he could see his Mom and Pops sitting in the second row.

The shepherds began singing: "They looked up and saw a star." All eyes on the stage looked up at him. Slowly, he lowered the star outward and then angled it downward. *Perfect, perfect*, he said to himself, leaning out a bit further.

Then, just as the song was ending, it happened. Suddenly down below, behind the scenery, someone bumped the ladder. Brian had a firm one-handed grip on the star pole, and he momentarily lost his balance. As his feet left the ladder, he wildly grabbed at a rope and, catching it, he and the star swung right through the shepherds' scene and off into the wings, landing with a thump.

Without losing a beat the Head Shepherd said, "Hark, I think I saw an angel fly by." The audience laughed and applauded as the curtains closed.

Everyone rushed to Brian and aside from having totally trashed the star, he was unhurt but a bit stunned. As the set was being changed for the last scene in the stable, Brian sat dejectedly in a chair backstage. *Yes*, he thought, *the old theatrical prediction caught up with me.* The star worked perfectly at rehearsal, but he'd sure messed up now.

Then there was Pops at his side. He had come backstage to check on Brian. "Well, the flying angel with the star will long be remembered! Everyone in the audience loved it."

"It wasn't planned that way, Pops," Brian insisted.

"You and I know that," said Pops, "but the audience thought it was the best part of the show. That was some special effect!"

"Well, I'm in real trouble now," whispered Brian. "The other thing I did perfectly at the rehearsal was 'The Bing Bong Carol Song.' I'll probably mess that up, too. Then everyone will hate me."

"Come on, Brian," said Pops. "We don't have to believe in that old story. Show them that it's only a fable by ringing that bell just the right way. You can do it!"

As Pops returned to his seat, Rob walked by with a smirk on his face and said, "What did I tell you?"

And then it was time for the last scene. Again everything was going right. The first graders sang without falling or fighting, the baby didn't cry, the shepherds entered with the proper awe, the crowns stayed firmly attached to the kings' heads, and even the lamb behaved perfectly.

Standing in the wings, Brian was ready as the group began singing "I Heard the Bells on Christmas Day." At the end of each line he was right on time with the bing bong. Time after time it was perfect.

And then the last line sounded in his ears as if the message was for him: "The wrong shall fail, the right prevail, with peace on earth, goodwill to men." *Yes, that's true*, thought Brian as he rang his bell with vigor and joy. He said aloud, "Yes, the right shall prevail!"

The curtains closed. The class cheered. The curtains opened for curtain calls and many bows. The cast accepted the applause and then all the stage crew came out on stage for more applause. Brian came out last, and everyone cheered the loudest for him. He had done it right!

As parents mingled and gathered their children, everyone told Brian what a great job he'd done. Maria told him that his flying scene was the most exciting thing she'd ever seen. Amanda said, "You really made 'The Bing Bong Carol Song' the highlight of the pageant. It was perfect."

Rob saw him in the parking lot later and came over to kid him: "You were really the star of the show. Get it, the star."

In the car going home, Pops said, "See, you've proved that a myth is just a myth. And I really liked that song about 'the wrong shall fail, the right prevail.' That's a good message."

The twins served their cookies, Mom and Pops sat on the sofa talking, and Brian thought about peace—not just on earth but in his home.

It was then that Brian noted that Pops had his arm around Mom. *Gee*, he thought, *that looks like the good old days!*

When it was time for bed, Brian hesitatingly asked: "Are you going to stay, Pops?"

"Well, your mom and I have some things to talk about. I'm taking her out to dinner tomorrow night. So we'll just have to see. You don't mind if we leave you alone tomorrow night?" Brian smiled.

So the next morning Brian called Amanda to say that he'd be at the cast party at her house that night.

It was a great party, and everyone was still talking about the flying angel and "The Bing Bong Carol Song." Coach and Miss Dombrowski were drinking fruit punch and laughing together. Mrs. Krebs let everyone hold the baby. Amanda asked Brian if he was going to be in the spring class play. He said maybe. But for now, he just hoped that peace on earth would come true at his house.

His folks came by the party around 10:30 to take him home. They were silent in the car and silent when they got in the door. Pops seemed to avoid talking to Brian by walking the sitter to her house down the block. Mom avoided him, too, by going upstairs to check on the twins, who were still awake and came running downstairs to hear about the party.

Pops returned and found them all in the living room, talking about the evening. Then Brian bravely changed the subject: "What happens tomorrow?"

Mom said with a smile, "It's the day we trim the tree."

"But first we're going to church together," added Pops. Everyone looked happy. Pops continued, "Then I'm going back to my apartment." Everyone looked sad. There was silence.

Then he added with a grin: "You can all come and help me pack up my things so I can move back in here." Everyone cheered and piled on Pops with hugs and kisses.

"I really missed you," he said quietly. "I now know that I need to be here with you all. We're going to have a good Christmas together."

And it was a good Christmas. They trimmed the tree, they went caroling with the neighbors, they took supper to a shut-in, they opened their packages on Christmas morning—a family again.

But best of all Brian felt he'd grown up a bit more. He thought about it a lot. He didn't have to believe in silly traditions. He could do things right—most of the time. He even figured they probably could be a family without two parents, although he sure liked having two much better.

He also hoped that Pops would never leave again and that he'd like his new job. And it seemed to him that even the twins were being more considerate and loving. And perhaps Mom wouldn't have to work such long hours and could do some things with them after school. Yes, the new year looked bright. He even thought he'd try out for the spring play.

In the days that followed Christmas he would often remember the words of the carol: "The wrong shall fail, the right prevail, with peace on earth, goodwill to men." And the bing bong in his heart seemed to say, "Right on!"

Sharing the Spirit

Illustration by Ludwig Richter, c. 1803.

Chapter Five

Sharing the Spirit

Reaching Out to Others with the True Meaning of Christmas

*I*n the rushed pace of a commercialized Christmas, the true meaning of this day is often lost. While each of us might describe this true meaning differently, there are common threads of caring, sharing, comforting, uplifting, and most of all, loving.

Reaching out beyond the confines of our own family lets us demonstrate an important aspect of Jesus' mission—to welcome all humankind into God's eternal family, a family that knows no boundaries. Ways of broadening our concept of family and of sharing love can take many forms.

There are many options for outreach. Be careful to choose those that fit with your family or group's interests, finances, and time. Save some ideas for other years. There are many Christmases ahead!

First, though, we need to ask ourselves some questions.

1. In reaching out to others, what does this group, family, or person (relative, friend, neighbor, stranger) need that I could supply?

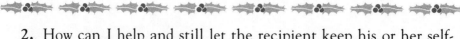

2. How can I help and still let the recipient keep his or her self-esteem and dignity?

3. What can our family give? Time, food, gifts, conversation, companionship, money, good ideas, a listening ear, physical help?

4. How can our outreach help bring us together as a family?

5. In helping, what do we expect from the recipient? If the recipient insists on giving us something in return, what might that be?

6. How does this outreach fit into our family schedule and budget?

Here's a list of outreach projects you might consider during the Christmas season:

✧ "Adopting" a family in need.

✧ Caroling at the homes of elderly persons and shut-ins or at adult-care facilities. When caroling to seniors or shut-ins, you may want to call in advance to say you're coming. (Some high school girls we know went caroling and found that an elderly woman was so alarmed by the noise that she called the police!) When walking the streets of a neighborhood, you may want to carry along some bells to announce your arrival.

✧ Making tray favors and visiting hospitals and other care facilities.

✧ Working as a volunteer on the team that serves holiday meals at a shelter for the homeless.

✧ Running errands, packing and mailing gifts, buying the tree for seniors or disabled folks in your neighborhood.

✧ Including singles and those without nearby family in some of your Christmas activities.

✧ Having a neighborhood party that includes everyone, not just the people you already know.

✧ Inviting a foreign or exchange student to spend Christmas day—or longer—with your family.

✧ Making a gingerbread house with a child whose parents both work.

✧ Telephoning people over the holidays—far-away relatives, former school teachers and coaches, friends and neighbors who have moved away.

✧ Encouraging children to make simple ornaments and give some of them to other children, teachers, and neighbors.

✦ Taking responsibility for the Christmas program at a school or church.

✦ Making extra batches of cookies and giving them to a busy young mother, a shut-in, the folks at the fire or police station, and so forth.

✦ Providing a supper for someone who finds it difficult to cook. Make it look festive and be sure to include a plate of Christmas cookies.

✦ Asking busy parents if you can babysit for them while they do Christmas shopping.

✦ Volunteering time at a school, a Boys or Girls Club, or church— supervising games, helping with a holiday party, providing food.

✦ Taking part in a community toy or food drive.

Most of the ideas on this list are self-explanatory, but four of them will be discussed in more detail here:

(1) "Adopting" a family in need;
(2) Planning a party for a youth group;
(3) Giving a large Christmas party at home; and
(4) Taking responsibility for a Christmas program at a school, church, or other large group.

Certainly these projects will take a good amount of time and planning, and you'll need the commitment, cooperation, and enthusiasm of many others. But if you call your family together and explain the project, you will find that they'll be supportive and helpful in sharing the spirit.

"Adopting" a Family in Need

This can be one of the most satisfying of your Christmas activities. Those who have chosen to do this say it has become a regular part of their Christmas celebration and that it is looked forward to by all the

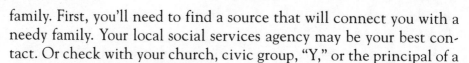

family. First, you'll need to find a source that will connect you with a needy family. Your local social services agency may be your best contact. Or check with your church, civic group, "Y," or the principal of a school in a low-income area.

If possible, adopt one specific family. Get information on the size of the family, names, ages of the children, and any special needs. This gives a focus to the activity and helps you to select the best things to give. If you have children, see if you can be matched with a family with children a little younger than yours.

Have a get-together with your family to talk about your plans. Use the term "Christmas Family" rather than "needy family." Decide the scope of your giving:

Are you going to provide Christmas dinner or enough food for several meals?

Do you have home furnishing items in good condition that you can share?

Will you buy a Christmas tree and provide some decorations?

Do your children have good out-grown clothing that could be passed along?

Do your children have toys to share?

How much money can the family budget spare to spend on new clothing, toys, and household gifts?

How much can each family member contribute from current allowances or savings?

Once you've decided how much you plan to do, make a list of everything you will need and also make a schedule for completing the project. Involve all family members in collecting the items—shopping, wrapping, packing, delivering. Set the delivery date and put it on your calendar.

Be sure that most food items are non-perishable. Don't forget personal gifts for the parents. And see that used items are clean and in working order.

Sometimes two families can work together to provide the essentials for a happy Christmas for another family. A school class or Scout troop can do the same thing. But it seems most meaningful when it is on the basis of one family's giving to another.

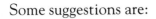

Some suggestions are:

Personal items: Sweaters and jackets, scarves and mittens, pretty lingerie, a dressy dress for a teen, long-sleeved shirts, boots, carry-alls, a wallet, cosmetics.

Household items: Blankets, small appliances, dishes and cookware, music cassettes.

Christmas decorations: A small tree, string of lights, ornaments, table candles, wreath.

Christmas dinner: (canned items or long-lasting produce) A whole canned chicken or ham, sweet potatoes, mashed potato mix, vegetables, cranberry sauce, cake mix, beverages, candy.

Other useful foods: Cereal, pancake mix, bread, non-perishable cheese, canned lunch meat, peanut butter, jam, granola bars, canned fruit, soups, canned meals (chili, hash, stew), crackers, cookies, popcorn, catsup, mayonnaise, sugar, flour, long-lasting produce such as potatoes, onions, apples.

You may find that some spare food items are in your own pantry. But in purchasing most of the food items, you'll have the opportunity to take the family shopping. It is both educational and fun to let them help find the non-perishable items. And you'll be amazed at the variety available.

A house walk-around can reap more gift items. Do it as a family. Go from room to room, from closet to cupboard to storage area, looking for things that your family no longer uses but still have life—games, books, kitchen equipment, linens, desk supplies. One family member can make a list, or, better yet, the item can be immediately moved to the place where you'll gather things for packing.

Start early to collect clothing items and allow time for washing and mending if needed. Ask friends to check their closets and drawers, too.

Buying new toys and clothing items is one of the best parts. Consider this question: "If you were to get just one Christmas gift, what would you want?" Books are excellent but are usually in second place to toys. Toys that can be played with for a length of time are better than ones that are just to be looked at. Many children don't get even one gift, so in your shopping be sure to select something truly special.

Finally, when you have all items ready, it's time to pack them so they look festive. Of course, you won't gift wrap the food, but you can decorate the cartons you put the food in, or put bows on the bags.

Pack used clothing items, household items, and decorations in three separate boxes. The gifts should be wrapped and labeled. If you don't know the child or adult's name, be sure to put an identifying label on the package, such as "toddler jacket," "size 14 sweater," "doll," "game for teen."

Depending on the rules set up by the social service group or agency, you will deliver your items directly to the family or take them to a headquarters that will make the delivery for you. Some Christmas families enjoy the social contact and find it a happy occasion, while others may feel embarrassed.

If you do have the opportunity to take your gifts directly to the recipients, don't plan a long visit. Let them know in advance that you are coming. If you have children going with you, prepare them ahead of time for what they may experience.

One year we learned that our Christmas family was from Samoa. Driving into a very low income area, we located the dilapidated apartment building. We unloaded the boxes of foods and gifts, each of us carrying part of the load.

It was an educational and emotional experience for our family. Hearing about such things or viewing them on television is not the same as actually seeing graffiti and rubbish, the lack of landscaping, the curious faces peeking out from behind apartment doors.

But we found the family of four to be a delightful group. Their tiny three-room apartment was immaculate, although quite bare. The children were shy at first, but the sight of the tree and gifts soon broke down the barriers. While we did not stay more than about fifteen minutes, the family was most gracious to us and insisted that we take home a large piece of Samoan tapa cloth, which we still enjoy today as a beautiful wall hanging.

The best part was seeing our children and theirs unpacking the gift items and putting them next to the yet-undecorated tree, all talking happily about Christmas.

From that day onward when we spoke of the poor and needy, we had a far better concept of sharing. And through the years since, our grown children have included outreach as part of their holiday activities and throughout the year.

Do not go into this project thinking that it will be something you can accomplish quickly. It is well worth your time and money, for what you do can make a real difference in the way another family experiences the important Christmas season.

Planning a Party for a Youth Group

A Christmas party doesn't have to be expensive, but it does have to be planned. Whether you are helping plan a party for a Boys or Girls Club, a day-care center, Scout group, or your own youngsters and their friends, there are four elements that make for success:

(1) festive decorations;
(2) food;
(3) activities; and
(4) "take homes" (prizes and favors).

Don't try to do all the work yourself—get the participation of other adults as well as the kids. Much of the preparation can actually take part at the party itself. For example, the party participants can help decorate the party area or make some of the food. That saves your time, but it also makes for fun.

Decorations

You may not have to spend any time on this if the party area already has a tree. However, here are some additional ideas.

1. Popcorn. As party givers know, party participants don't all arrive at the same time. That's where popcorn comes in. Of course, popcorn is a good "munchie," but it can also be strung to hang on the tree. Little children like to put strings of it around their necks, too. Older kids can use it to festoon the tree or to hang from wall to wall. And after the party, strings of it can be taken home and used there for decoration.

2. Tree trimming. Even if there is a decorated tree on hand, obtain a small one (about 3' tall is ideal) for trimming at the party. If you tell the tree-lot attendant or manager that you are giving the tree to a shut-in (which you will), you will probably be given a free tree. Trees don't have to be a perfect shape—they all look great when trimmed. Gather supplies for making ornaments—Styrofoam balls, shiny paper, wide-tip marking pens, beads, glitter, and the like. Let each party guest make an ornament for the tree. After the party, take the tree to a shut-in or someone else who would appreciate a small tree. If possible, let the kids go along to deliver it.

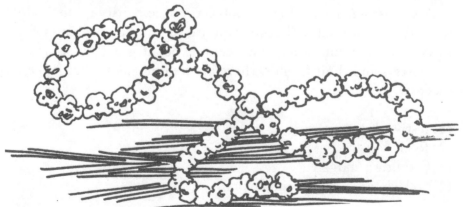

3. Balloons. Ask your party shop for a good price on their least expensive balloons. Divide the participants into teams of two or three and give each team five balloons. Have a race to see which team can get their balloons blown up and tied off, tied together with a ribbon, and ready to hang. An adult may have to help with the hanging. Everyone gets to take home a balloon at the end of the party.

4. Small wreaths. Get a bundle of greens at the Christmas tree lot. Provide each youngster with a metal clothes hanger. Show how to bend the hanger into a circle, keeping the curved hook intact. Distribute greens. Let kids cut them into 6"-8" pieces. Using narrow, inexpensive red or green ribbon, bind the greens to the hanger, piece by piece, until the hanger is covered. Decorate with a bow. The wreaths can be used as decorations at the party and may then be taken home.

5. Santas and angels. Get a wide roll of butcher paper, blank newsprint, wrapping paper, or other inexpensive paper. Cut the paper into 6' lengths, one for each child. Put the paper on the floor and have each child lie down on the paper as another youngster uses a pencil to draw an outline around his or her body. With wide-tip marking pens, each one then fills in and adds to her or his outline so as to make it look like a Santa Claus, a Mrs. Claus, or an angel. Let the children sign their drawings and hang them up around the room.

Food

Simple or hearty—depending on the time of the party—the foods should have a festive look. The first things we think of at this season is cookies, but here's a variety of choices:

1. Cookies. If time permits and you have large kitchen facilities, let participants take part in the making of sugar cookies, shortbread, or other simple cookies. Or you may make the cookies ahead. Or you can buy plain cookies (vanilla wafers, gingersnaps, shortbread) and then have red and green icing and sprinkles on hand so the kids can decorate the cookies.

2. Cupcakes. These are easier to eat than pieces of cake. They can be made at the party or in advance. Divide the batter of a white cake mix in half and use non-toxic food coloring to make half the batter green and half red. Filling each muffin cup with some of each color makes Christmasy cupcakes. Let everyone help decorate the tops.

3. Snowmen. Gather these supplies: bags of big marshmallows, toothpicks, raisins, drained maraschino cherries, black paper, and scissors. Using the toothpicks and three marshmallows, show the youngsters how to put together a snowman. Use scissors to make the middle and top "balls" a little smaller (the scraps can be eaten!). Raisins make good buttons and eyes. (Use a toothpick to poke a small hole, then push in the raisin.) A piece of a cherry (poked in place with a toothpick) can make the mouth. The black paper can be fashioned into a stove-pipe hat. These snowmen can be eaten immediately, used as table favors/place cards, or kept as a "take home."

4. Christmas Tree Sandwiches. Using a large cookie cutter in the shape of a Christmas tree, cut bread for sandwiches. (Some bakeries have red or green bread during the holidays.) Spread with favorite fillings or cheese for grilling. You can use two different fillings between three pieces of bread. If using peanut butter as a filling, freeze the bread in advance for easier spreading.

5. Strawberry Applesauce. For a festive fruit, mix in a blender two cans of applesauce with a package of frozen sliced strawberries. Put in small individual dishes and add a bright green mint leaf for garnish.

6. Hot Dog Roll Ups. Use crescent-shaped refrigerated biscuits as wrappers for the hot dogs. Spread each piece of unrolled dough with a small amount of chili sauce. Then lay the hot dog and a piece of cheese at the wide end and roll up. Place on a baking sheet with the tail end of the biscuit dough on the bottom so it can't unroll. Bake in a 375 degree oven until biscuits are nicely browned. Garnish by putting a small sprig of green parsley in each end of the roll up.

7. Layered Gelatin Salad. Make this salad the day before. For 12-16 servings, you will need two large boxes of gelatin—one cherry or berry, the other lime or lemon tinted with green food coloring. Prepare the two large boxes of gelatin according to package instructions, except reduce liquid by one quarter cup. Add fruit if you desire. Using a large mold or rectangular glass dish, pour in the green gelatin and refrigerate until firm. This will take several hours. (Don't put the red gelatin in the refrigerator.) Mix a large package of cream cheese with one-fourth cup powdered sugar, adding a tablespoon of milk at a time until it has the consistency of frosting. (You'll use two to four tablespoons in all.) Spread over the firm green gelatin. Then pour the red gelatin on top and refrigerate until firm. Just before serving, sprinkle very lightly with coconut to decorate.

Activities

Depending on the age of the youngsters, you'll have dancing, caroling, and/or games. Here are some fun and easy games.

1. Pin the Nose on Rudolph. Using butcher paper or shelf paper, draw a simple outline of a reindeer, about 3' tall. Then cut out of red paper as many 2" round circles as there will be players. Then play the game just as you would "Pin the Tail on the Donkey."

2. Bobbing for Apples. Use both red and green apples so the tub of water looks festive. Teens like this game. Time each participant and see who can most quickly bend over the tub (hands behind back) and retrieve an apple using only the teeth.

3. Christmas Relay. Buy, borrow, or make two Santa hats. Also have two pairs of really large boots or galoshes. Divide the group into two teams and have each team form a line. Give a hat and boots to the first person in each line. At the "Go" the person puts on the hat and the boots, shouts "Ho! Ho! Ho!" then takes off the hat and boots and gives them to the next person on the team, who repeats the actions. The last person in line must take the hat and boots back to the first person, who again puts them on and says "Ho! Ho! Ho!" The first team to complete this wins the game.

4. *In-house Scavenger Hunt for Older Kids.* Divide the group into pairs and give out a prepared-in-advance list of clues for items that can be seen around the house or meeting room. Give each pair a pencil so they can note the name and location of the item. The first pair to complete the list in the time-limit wins. A sample list follows. The answers to the clues are in parentheses, but do not write them on your own list.

It goes 'round and 'round. (wreath)
It led three people. (star)
It announces Christmas Day in Bethlehem. (bell)
It has wings but doesn't make a nest. (angel)
It doesn't need an arrow. (bow)
It's not to be peeked into. (package)
It is usually made of snow. (cotton ball)
It was better than the inn. (nativity scene)
It makes a joyful sound. (Christmas recording or cassette)
It comes from near and far. (Christmas card)
It never lasts long. (Christmas cookie)
It does not point. (poinsettia)
It drives folks nuts. (nutcracker)
It tells the whole story. (Bible)
It gets dragged indoors in England. (yule log)
It has more to do with lips than toes. (mistletoe)
It is for a giant to wear. (Christmas stocking)

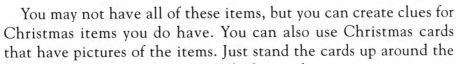

You may not have all of these items, but you can create clues for Christmas items you do have. You can also use Christmas cards that have pictures of the items. Just stand the cards up around the house where they can be seen easily during the game.

You may find other party ideas at your local public library, where you will find many books on party games. There are sure to be several that will adapt well to the age group at your party.

"Take-homes"

No one should go home empty handed from a Christmas party. Perhaps you have already provided a "take-home" from the above activities: a string of popcorn, a balloon, or a marshmallow snowman. You can also provide a "take-home" from this list.

1. Personalized Ornament. Buy a box of the least expensive, plain-colored ornaments. (Don't get ones with a shiny finish.) With a marking pen, carefully write the name of each youngster on an ornament. Or let the youngsters use glue and glitter to put their names on ornaments for taking home.

2. Red and Green Lollipops—always a favorite.

3. Photographs. In advance of the party, make red and green construction-paper frames. During the party, use an instant camera to take pictures of each child in action. Put the pictures in the frames.

4. Plastic-wrapped Cookie. Using icing, decorate large cookies with the name of each youngster. When the icing is dry, wrap the cookie in colored plastic wrap.

5. Christmas Stickers. Provide a variety for kids to choose from.

6. Unisex Bracelets. The popular woven bracelets are easy to make in advance or even at the party. Try them in red and green.

7. *Shiny Stars*. Using mylar or foil and cardboard, make each youngster a star to hang in a window or on his or her bedroom door.

The last five minutes of the party should be "put-away time." Organize partygoers to take food to the kitchen, fold up chairs, take down balloons, pick up rubbish, and so on. That way, when the party's over, it's over, and you can get on to the next holiday event.

Giving a Christmas Carol Party

The joyous music of Christmas makes the best kind of party for adults, or adults and children. Many folks take part in caroling at church or at sing-along *Messiah* concerts.

However, being invited for a dinner at a home and then singing carols can be the highlight of the season for many—especially those who no longer have family nearby for Christmas Eve and Christmas Day celebrations.

* **Select the date.** Because the holidays are a busy time, choose your date well in advance. The weekend nights before Christmas are the most desirable. Give yourself ample time to prepare for the party so you can enjoy it, too.

* Make the guest list. Be as inclusive as your home will allow. This event is enjoyed by young and old, and it works best if there are several generations present. Try to include new neighbors and friends who may not have many other social engagements.

* Send invitations early. As soon as Thanksgiving is concluded, get your invitations in the mail. Be sure to ask for a response (and give a date for the response) so you'll know how many will attend. Specify attire—the phrase "Festive Dress" lets people wear glittery pant suits, red jackets with green slacks, and a variety of comfortable party clothes. Let folks know on the invitation that you welcome their help: in solo singing, in group singing, in preparing part of the meal, or bringing homemade cookies. Keep an accurate list of what each one has offered to do.

* Find the accompanist. Piano, guitar, electronic keyboard, recorded music—those are some of your options. Piano accompaniment—or an electronic keyboard—is most common; if you don't have an in-house pianist, be sure to find one right away. Sometimes you can find a competent accompanist through a music teacher, your church, or a school music department.

* Plan the menu. Write down what you plan to serve. It's a good idea to begin with a serve-yourself punch bowl and a simple appetizer that isn't too filling. This leaves you free to greet guests. A make-ahead casserole dish and hot bread are easy for you to do. Let others bring the salads, vegetables, or plates of homemade cookies. One easy, but festive, salad dish is sliced red crab apples arranged with green minted pear halves.

After caroling, serve ice cream and toppings for make-your-own sundaes to go with the cookies others have brought. Everyone enjoys sampling a variety of cookies!

* Decide on logistics. If parking isn't sufficient, give suggestions for additional parking places in the invitation. See if you have the needed number of dishes, cutlery, and table linens. Or use Christmasy paper and plastic. Decide whether the meal will be eaten "in the lap" or whether you have adequate tables and chairs for seating. You may choose a combination.

* Choose a theme. Just singing favorite carols can be an adequate theme. But you may want to add some of these "bells and whistles."

1. When people RSVP, ask them the names of their favorite carols. "Dedicate" (announce the persons' names) before singing each favorite carol.

2. Make it an old-fashioned Christmas with food of one nationality: Swedish, Italian, German, Mexican, and so forth. For example, at an Old English Christmas, you'd serve roast beef and Yorkshire pudding at dinner and have trifle for dessert. A festive south-of-the-border supper can include chicken enchiladas and salads. Each nationality has interesting foods to choose from. The food should be hearty, but it needn't be costly. You may want to use some of the recipes from around the world, featured in chapter 6.

3. Include with the caroling the reading of the Christmas story from the Bible. Thus after reading about angels you'll sing angel carols, such as "Hark! the Herald Angels Sing"; and when you read of kings you'll sing "We Three Kings," and so forth. Choose in advance those who will do the Bible readings. Tell them which verses they'll need to read so they can practice at home if they wish. You'll find selected readings from the Bible in chapter 8.

4. Borrow slides or pictures of the Holy Land or of Europe from the library and use them as illustrations between songs.

5. Have a guest artist. Music schools may have vocalists, a harpist, or instrumentalists who would enjoy doing some solos between the group singing. Sometimes a church has a group of bell ringers who will play for a small donation.

6. Use the story "The Search for Christmas" at the end of this chapter as the framework for the carols you plan to sing.

* **Make a time schedule to include all the arrangements.** Assign tasks to yourself and your helpers and note on the calendar when they should be done.

1. *Make the food.* Choose an appetizer and a casserole that can be prepared ahead—the day before or even a few weeks before and frozen. Most casseroles freeze extremely well. Get your part of the food preparation done well in advance of the party day.

2. *Decorate the house.* With the help of family or friends, get this accomplished at least a week before the party. Don't forget decorations for the kitchen, the powder room, the closet or bedroom (the place where coats are often put).

3. *Get song sheets.* You can buy booklets with the words to songs, but the cheapest way is to type out the words—*ones that are in the public domain only!*—and make many copies of them. Number each carol to help the singers find the exact song quickly. These song sheets are never out of date, so keep them from year to year.

4. *Plan the serving table.* Get out the utensils, serving dishes, and trivets for hot dishes. Make a little card for the dishes that will be brought: "Susie Simmons's salad," "Mike Woo's cookies," and so forth. Everyone likes credit, and it's fun to know who brought what. Set out plates, napkins, and utensils for the buffet.

5. *Set up tables and chairs, table decorations, and glasses.* Assign someone (not you) to put ice and water in glasses as the guests are gathering.

6. *Go over your program.* Make sure that you and the accompanist know the order of the carols.

7. *Make guest assignments.* Some will have already volunteered to bring salads, cookies, or some other part of the meal. Let one or two be assigned as ice cream servers. Others will have volunteered to sing special songs. The remaining ones will have jobs like moving chairs, handing out song sheets or candles, or participating in special carols as explained in the next section.

* **Plan your program.** Consider adding to the fun of caroling by having "audience" participation. These carols work well:

"We Three Kings." Let three men (or women, as queens) sing the three verses and everyone else the choruses.

"*Jingle Bells.*" Have some bells and ask certain people to come forward and ring along with the chorus. Also play the song through once with only bell ringing. This is a good assignment for nonsingers.

"*O Holy Night.*" There is usually a soprano or tenor who loves to solo here. If not, choose two to four of your best singers.

"*The Friendly Beasts.*" Each beast's part is sung by a different person. Kids love this one.

"*Away in a Manger.*" This song can be sung by those under age eighteen.

"*Deck the Halls.*" Let the "fa la la" parts be sung by men in the first verse and women in the second verse. Select a men's leader and a women's leader to get the men and women to stand up for each "fa la la."

"*O Tannenbaum*" ("*O Christmas Tree*"). Ask those who can sing in German to come forward and do so, and then join with everyone in singing the English version.

"*Silent Night.*" End the caroling by singing this carol by the light of the Christmas tree, or by candlelight. Give each person a candle to hold and stand in a circle to sing two verses. Then continue humming the carol as the candles are extinguished one by one around the circle.

* **Prepare for the production number.** "The Twelve Days of Christmas" makes an amusing production number. You will need to gather the props ahead of time. Choose in advance fourteen extroverts and tell them to meet after supper to get their props and orders. (One person will be assigned leader to get the group somewhat organized. Because Day Two requires two people, you'll need thirteen actors plus the leader.)

The action described below takes place only when the particular day is mentioned. Thus the partridge will perform twelve times and the fiddler only once. The actors stand with their backs to the audience (who does all the singing), each one keeping his or her costume/action/prop secret until turning around the first time mentioned. They then face the audience but repeat their action each time thereafter.

1. A Partridge in a Pear Tree. Have a tree branch with a paper cutout of a bird tied firmly to one branch.

2. Two Turtle Doves. Use two people for this (one man, one woman), preferably a kissy couple. Paint a large lipstick kiss on the cheek of the man. The woman pretends to kiss it each time.

3. *Three French Hens*. This actor tucks her hands under her arms (like wings) and calls "Oui, oui" each time.

4. *Four Calling Birds*. This person uses a telephone or a megaphone to "call."

5. *Five Gold Rings*. String together five large, brass drapery rings for holding high and jingling.

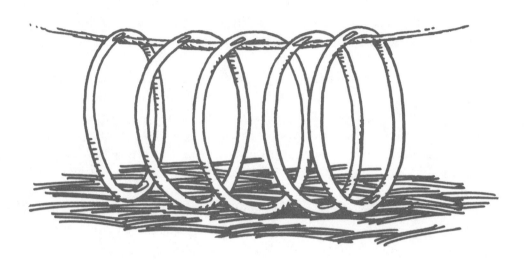

6. *Six Geese A-laying*. Provide one uncooked and two hard-boiled eggs for this person, who stands on a newspaper. Each time the line is sung, the actor juggles the two hard-boiled eggs. (The uncooked egg is in the actor's pocket.) For the second to the last round (#11) the actor will switch the one fresh egg with one of the hard-boiled ones and "accidently" drop it (on the newspaper). For the final round (#12) the actor again juggles the two hard-boiled eggs and tosses one out toward someone in the audience, who will probably duck, thinking it is an uncooked egg.

7. *Seven Swans A-swimming*. Dress this person in swim fins, face mask, and snorkel. Or let him or her take off an article of apparel each time, down to a bathing suit.

8. *Eight Maids A-milking*. Fill a rubber glove with water and tie it securely. The person "milks" the glove and in the last round holds up a milk carton.

9. *Nine Pipers Piping.* Any musical horn or kazoo will do here. The person should give a blast on the instrument each time introduced—(rounds #9 through #12).

10. *Ten Ladies Dancing.* Use a willing child for this part. Provide ballet or tap shoes and a frilly tutu. A pirouette or dance step should be done each round, starting with #10.

11. *Eleven Lords A-leaping.* Give this person a jump rope or a hula hoop, or let him hold his nose as if jumping into water.

12. *Twelve Fiddlers Fiddling.* A violin, guitar, or ukelele will suffice here. This person has only one turn to act.

* **Make name tags for a large party.** Along with the persons' names, write in the lower corner their volunteer assignment: salad maker, cookie baker, ice cream server, king, twelve days production, bell ringer, "Fa la la" chorus, and so forth. Go for 100 percent participation. If you run out of assignments, consider these: leader of applause, table clearing chairman, chair folder-upper, dishwasher loader.

* **Have an ice-breaker for the beginning of the party.** If you won't be serving dinner right away, all can play the icebreaker while having punch and an appetizer. Here are three ideas:

1. *A Guessing Game.* Put Christmas candies in a large glass container. Be sure to count how many you put in. Place the container on a table with pencils and paper. Let everyone guess. The closest answer gets a prize.

2. *Favorite Carols.* Give each person a pencil and a list of those attending the party. Before supper, each guest must find each person on the list and ask the person's favorite carol, writing it opposite that person's name. The first one with a completed list gets a prize. And a social bonus—all the guests have met one another.

3. *In-house Scavenger Hunt.* See page 122 for this game, which is sure to keep the guests moving.

Now that you see some of the possibilities, you can plan your own party. Be sure to write on your calendar the preparations that need to be done in advance of the party day.

A Christmas party is not an overwhelming undertaking if planned in advance. You need to start early and do a little each day. And the results are well-worth the effort!

Presenting a Christmas Carol Program

A framework for carol singing helps to focus the group on each carol and its special message. The following "script" can be used for a home, church, or school program. It can be adapted for use with just one person: the storytelling narrator. It can be modified as a play for several characters. Or it can be acted out by the characters as the narrator reads the story.

It can also be used without music as a story to tell to children. Although the story is about children, it will also be enjoyed by adults at a Christmas carol gathering.

The length of this program is adjustable. Already included are the most popular carols, but you can add other favorites. While the script as is can be used as two thirty-minute sections with an intermission in the middle, it can be shortened to as little as one forty-minute program by taking out carols, singing only one verse, or deleting an entire section—some text and a song—such as the trips to Poland, Spain, or the American Midwest. Read it aloud once, timing how long it takes you to read the text. Then add an average of forty-five seconds for each carol verse, since you'll want to sing several verses of some and only one verse of others. This should give you a good idea of the length of your program.

The Search for Christmas: A Program of Carol Singing

NARRATOR:

This is a story about searching—searching for something so important that it led to an exciting journey for a boy and his friends. The boy's name was David, and he lived in Yorkshire, England, where his father was a turkey farmer on land that had once been part of a large estate. In fact, the grand manor house was still occupied by Lord and Lady Filbert, who rented the land to the small farmers.

Early one winter, David was walking in the field when he saw Lord Filbert bent over a trap, looking at a dog whose paw had been caught. Lord Filbert raised his gun to put the dog out of its misery, but David stopped him and begged to have the dog for his own. Lord Filbert gave in, and soon the dog was well enough to follow David everywhere. Even though it was a small cowardly dog, David decided to call him Goliath.

The day before Christmas Eve, David's mother sent him to the village to buy wheat flour, squash, and plums for her Christmas cooking. David sometimes grumbled about having to work hard with his father, so he was happy to go to town. The walk was much easier than moving hay around in the old turkey house or watching over his baby brother, who was so mischievous that he often got David into trouble.

As David and Goliath slogged through the snow, they soon could hear music coming from the village. On the corner by the pub, three tattered men were singing "Please Put a Penny in the Old Man's Hat."

(SONG: *"Please Put a Penny in the Old Man's Hat"*)

Although his parents had very little extra money, David had been taught to help those who had even less, and he felt pleased to put three pennies into the hat. Then, as he passed the old stone church, he heard more music and went in to listen. The choir was rehearsing for their Christmas Eve program. It was warm inside, and David and Goliath curled up on a back pew out of sight and listened to "O Come, All Ye Faithful."

(SONG: "O Come, All Ye Faithful")

Right in the middle of the carol, Goliath joined in with a loud, off-key howl. The choir master stopped the singing and turned to see the interlopers. He shouted at David, "Begone you and your odd dog—and put some money in the collection box to atone for spoiling our practice."

Goliath had his tail between his legs, and David had his head down, but they followed orders by going to the collection box—another three pennies gone.

Outside in the cold, they headed toward the grocer's, but on the way they smelled something so delicious that even Goliath began to run faster, sniffing the air. It was the smell of chestnuts roasting—the sign that Christmas was really coming.

(SONG: "The Christmas Song" ["Chestnuts Roasting on an Open Fire"])

Sitting next to a man huddled by the fire was a sad-faced girl David had seen at school. David said to the man, "Three chestnuts, sir; one for me, one for Goliath, and one for her," pointing to the girl.

The man snapped: "Don't you give her nothing, she's a bad girl." But he took David's money for three chestnuts, giving two to David and putting one in his own pocket, saying, "I'll give it to her later."

David didn't want to argue and walked on to the shop where there were turkeys hanging in the window, beef and kidney pies on the shelves, and large crocks filled with mincemeat. He told Goliath to sit by the lamppost while he went inside, and he gave Goliath one of his two chestnuts. Goliath loved it!

David announced what his mother wanted and held out the money that he had left. The shop owner looked at the coins and laughed, "For that, lad, you get one plum and one spoon of flour." In shame, David left the store. What could he possibly tell his mother? He then noticed that the girl from the chestnut stand was sitting in the cold, huddled next to Goliath.

"I'm sorry," she said, "your dog was warm, and I was so cold. I wanted to thank you for the chestnut." David also offered her the last chestnut he'd kept for himself and asked, "Why did your father say you were a bad girl?"

Walking along next to him, she said, "Because I'd rather read books than pick chestnuts. I forgot I was to help him because I was reading such a good book. Oh, maybe you don't remember me from school—my name is Lucia." He looked puzzled at the name. "My mum is from Sweden, and I was named after Lucia, the Queen of Light in the Swedish celebration. Don't you just love Christmas?"

David said, "I'm not sure," and told her how he had spent almost all the food money. Just then they passed the manor house, where carolers were singing at the big front door while Lord and Lady Filbert beamed at them.

(SONG: "God Rest Ye Merry, Gentlemen")

By the time the three reached the little farm, David had decided to put off facing his mother by showing Lucia the turkey coops. Inside the hay smelled so good. They were cold from the walk and sat down on either side of Goliath to share his warmth.

Lucia stroked the dog and said, "Sometimes I like animals better than people. People only think about buying and selling, but animals seem to know the true meaning of Christmas. That's why the animals were there when Jesus was born. Did you know that?"

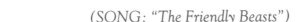

(SONG: "The Friendly Beasts")

As the last rays of the sun slanted into the high windows of the coop, David and Lucia felt drowsy. David muttered, "I wonder how turkeys feel about Christmas."

Before Lucia could answer, a voice said, "I'll tell you—it's *no* fun." They turned to find a large turkey beside them. "It's no fun if the lady of the manor has her eye on you for Christmas dinner. There's no such thing as a happy Christmas for turkeys!"

Goliath surprised them all by adding, "It won't be happy for me, either. When I get a bone, that big sheepdog at the manor house takes it away from me."

"And after what I've just done with the food money, it won't be a happy time for me either," said David.

"Nor for me," said Lucia sadly. "If the spirit of Christmas isn't here, I wonder where we could find the real Christmas."

The turkey replied, "I don't know, but we could search for it."

"Just who are you?" asked David, "And when can we leave?"

The turkey snapped, "Who am I? You dunce, I'm Tom, Tom Turkey, and I'm ready when you are—but where are we going?"

"To Bethlehem," said David. "That's where it all began." So Lucia and David, with Goliath in his arms, climbed on Tom's back and were off in search of Christmas.

Into the starry night they flew, across the English channel, across the continent of Europe. Suddenly Lucia cried, "David, look, it's so beautiful—there below, it must be Bethlehem."

(SONG: "O Little Town of Bethlehem")

Tom landed them gently in a field where shepherds were watching their flocks. On the nearby road, they joined the pilgrims who were walking along. Among them were three elegantly dressed gentlemen whose servants were leading camels loaded with gifts. Lucia nudged David and said, "They've got to be kings!"

David's eyes grew wide. "But that was centuries ago!" he said. Suddenly the three men began to sing.

(SONG: "We Three Kings")

As they reached the Church of the Nativity and made their way through the incense-filled chapels and down the stone steps, they finally came to the place where the manger was supposed to have rested almost 2,000 years before. A choir of school children was standing nearby, singing.

(SONG: "Away in a Manger")

But the sad faces of the children showed that all those years had not changed Bethlehem. The country still echoed with hatred among Christians, Arabs, and Jews. "The real Christmas doesn't seem to be here," said Lucia.

As they walked back to the shepherds' field, David saw a beautiful stone on the ground. It sparkled as if stars were inside it. He picked it up and carefully put it in his pocket.

Near the field, they heard the shepherds singing softly and looking up at the stars.

(SONG: "The First Noel")

Tom Turkey was sitting in a low tree branch. As they all climbed back aboard, Tom lifted them quickly into the air. The lights of the town looked like diamonds as Tom flew ever higher. Lucia said they were so high they could easily hear the angels sing.

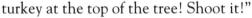

(SONG: "Hark! The Herald Angels Sing")

"Maybe the powerful cities of Europe know about the real Christmas," David said. Tom agreed to take them to some cities where Christmas was being celebrated. Besides, Tom said he needed some refueling.

Soon Tom was swooping down, having spotted a grain bin at a farm in Poland. They landed with a bump, and Tom dumped them off. As he gobbled the grain, the children hid behind a haystack and listened to a conversation between a king and his page.

(SONG: "Good King Wenceslas")

No sooner had they left Poland than Tom landed again, this time in Germany. "I need a second course," he said, landing at the very top of a large Christmas tree in the town square. Far below the townspeople were singing.

(SONG: "O Tannenbaum"/"O Christmas Tree")

During the singing, David saw many trays of decorated Christmas cookies under the tree. He slid down quietly, took one for each of them, slipped an extra one into his pocket, and scrambled back up the tree.

Just at that moment, someone in the square shouted, "Look, a turkey at the top of the tree! Shoot it!"

Tom flapped his wings for take-off, saying, "I don't want to be turkey sandwiches for those folks. Let's get out of here!"

They were off once more but soon saw the lights of a beautiful city and a huge building bright with festive decorations. "That's La Scala, the

famous opera house," said Lucia. "I've read about it in my books. They are rehearsing for tomorrow evening's Christmas program. Let's go inside!"

Tom obliged by flying in an open window, and they all huddled in the topmost balcony while the famous diva sang.

(SONG: "Bring a Torch Jeannette, Isabella")

After she finished, they peeked out the high windows. Outside the glittering building, poor people begged for coins. Lucia said sadly, "Even in a great city of Europe, where we've heard such beautiful music, we haven't found the real Christmas."

David answered, "Maybe we could look for it in America."

"All right!" said Tom. "That's my home country. I can take you there, but it's a long ocean crossing and we'll need a little help from the angels."

(SONG: "Angels We Have Heard on High")

In a surprisingly short time, Tom, slightly out of breath, said, "There's New York City—I can land over in that clearing in Central Park." Soon the group was on the ground and running happily down the brightly lighted streets. No one in New York thought a boy, a girl, a dog, and a turkey were a strange sight. They joined some folks who were gathered on a street corner, singing about city sidewalks.

(SONG: "Silver Bells")

"This isn't really Christmas," said Tom. "Let me show you where America was born—in beautiful New England. I need to rest, but I have friends who will take you for a sleigh ride in the country." Soon Tom swooped down on a big sleigh. Silently they landed in the back, unobserved by the others enjoying the ride through the winter wonderland of the snowy countryside.

(SONG: "Winter Wonderland")

When the ride was over, David said, "I know America is a big country—do we have time to see more?"

Tom replied, "Now that I've had a nap I'm going to take you to the Midwest." Leaving the sleigh riders behind, they flew at a low altitude—so low they could see children rolling the deep snow into large balls.

As they landed, Goliath looked at the snowballs. "I love balls, but I'm afraid those are too big for me to fetch. Tom, why don't you and I confer on the remainder of the trip, while you two kids go and help make a snowman."

(SONG: "Frosty the Snowman")

As soon as David and Lucia finished the snowman, Goliath and Tom had the plan ready. They were going to fly over the Rocky Mountains to a little school in the Pacific Northwest. They arrived in time to watch sweet-faced kindergartners practicing a song for their pageant. They had lined up on stage holding clusters of small silver bells, which they rang while singing.

(SONG: "Jingle Bells")

When the pageant was over, Lucia said, "As long as we've come this far, I want to see southern California."

As they walked across the schoolyard talking about their next stop, David spotted a small bell left on the ground. He put it in his pocket as he argued, "What do southern Californians know about Christmas—they don't even have snow!"

Tom made a turkey smile and said wisely, "I'll take you there anyway—just for fun. You know, they may not have snow, but they do sing about it."

(SONG: "Let It Snow")

Not to be out-done, Goliath said, "One of the most famous Christmas songs tells how they feel about Christmas without snow in the city of Los Angeles."

"How do you know that?" asked Lucia.

Goliath said shyly, "Oh, I had a friend named Lassie who told me about the song called 'White Christmas.'" And soon, they were flying over the city of Los Angeles, looking down at palm trees and beaches.

(SONG: "White Christmas")

When the song was over, Lucia sighed and said, "How sad that everyone is looking for a special, perfect Christmas—and are not finding it."

David replied, "We looked for the real Christmas in Bethlehem, and it wasn't there. Then we looked in some important cities of Europe, but it wasn't there. And we thought it might be in the adventure of America, but as wonderful as all these visits were, the real meaning of Christmas wasn't there."

Goliath added, "And I'm tired of travel. I'd sure like to go home—now."

Tom snapped, "You know, I'm not a private jet or a reindeer; I'm just one big hunk of a turkey. I'll need help to get you all the way home."

"How will you do it?" asked David.

"Just watch and listen," replied Tom. And with that he gave a whistle, and what should appear but that most famous team of reindeer.

(SONG: "Rudolph, the Red-Nosed Reindeer")

So, instead of Rudolph and friends pulling a sleigh, Tom was hitched up to the last reindeer, and when everyone was aboard they snuggled down for the long trip. Soon they were talking about what they hoped would be in their Christmas stockings when they got home.

Lucia spoke first: "I don't want even one toy, just books, and the only other thing I want is peace. I'd like peace—peace in our town and peace with my dad about my book reading."

Then it was David's turn: "I'd like peace with Lord Filbert. I wish he'd stop picking on me and on my dog and on my family."

Goliath added, "And I'd like peace with that big old sheepdog who lives at the manor house. What about you, Tom?"

The turkey replied, "Well, you know what happens to turkeys. I imagine they're looking for me right now. If the clock on the tower we just passed is correct, it will be Christmas Eve morning when we get home. It's already midnight, and soon the Christmas story will begin again."

(SONG: "It Came Upon the Midnight Clear")

As they drifted into sleep, the reindeer flew onward. Suddenly there was a jolt, and the sleeping group awoke with a start. David sat up in the straw. Goliath lifted his head. Lucia rubbed her eyes. Tom stretched his neck.

Lucia spoke excitedly, "How long were we gone? If it's Christmas Eve, I have to do the baking."

David looked puzzled, "I don't know if we've been gone at all."

Goliath and Tom were silent.

As Lucia ran off toward home, she said, "Look for me when I come caroling with my friends. We'll sing one of my favorite songs at your door. Listen to how it goes."

(SONG: "Here We Come A-Wassailing")

With Goliath tagging along behind him, David hurried to his house. As his mother hugged him, he explained how he had hid in the turkey shed because he was so ashamed to have spent the money she'd given him for the holiday food. She wasn't upset—in fact she hugged him again for sharing the money with others who needed it.

She then explained that they'd have plenty of food because Lord and Lady Filbert had just decided to have a feast for the entire village.

"There will be roasts and hams and turkey—and that much turkey will be good business for us," she said. Thinking of Tom, David didn't like the sound of that, but his mum continued, "We're invited to help decorate the manor house today. In fact, Father is cutting the yule log right now."

(SONG: "Deck the Halls")

As they were hanging strings of holly across the great room of the manor, Lord Filbert called David aside. He said he had heard that David was a very good student, and the schoolmaster had said he was excellent with figures. Would he like to come once a week and help Lord Filbert with his records? David was thrilled—his first real job! He immediately said yes! What a wonderful Christmas present—and from an unexpected source!

Later that night, David and Lucia sat together in the big church waiting for the Christmas Eve service to begin. He told her about his job, and she told him that her father had come home with Christmas gifts and that some were just the right shapes to be books!

Then, the service in the old stone building began with "O Holy Night."

(SONG: "O Holy Night")

Soon the minister was reading from the Gospels the story of Jesus' birth. David's eyes wandered upward, and he saw Tom roosting high in the rafters. He was glad to see that the bird was safe for this holiday season—and probably spared forever because he would soon be too tough to eat.

And from under his pew came the thumping of Goliath's tail. All was well.

As the service ended, the bells rang from the tower. It was midnight. Christmas Day had come.

(SONG: "I Heard the Bells on Christmas Day")

The choir led the way out into the cold night. Arm in arm with her father, Lucia turned to say goodnight. The man smiled at David and wished him a merry Christmas. Could this be the same man who had been so gruff the day before? David decided that from then on he would not judge people so quickly.

Everyone was exchanging Christmas greetings and starting to walk toward their homes. The sounds of "Merry Christmas" and "Happy New Year" echoed in the clear, star-filled night.

(SONG: "We Wish You a Merry Christmas")

As David walked along the road with his parents, his father carrying his little brother, he realized how much he loved his family, his beloved dog, his pet turkey, and his new friend, Lucia. Maybe this was the real Christmas—a Christmas not found in creeds or history or power or wealth but in love. On that cold night, he felt all warm inside. He felt happy at last. It wasn't just that Jesus had come to the world years ago; it was that Jesus had come to him this year—in love, in caring, and in joy. With his family, he sang all the way home.

(SONG: "Joy to the World")

Later, tucked in bed under his quilt, David remembered everything that had happened to him. Or did it really happen? He decided it was just a dream. Then he remembered the little treasures he'd put in his jacket pocket. He slipped out of bed to see if they were still there. And they were! The sparkling rock from the shepherds' field—his dad would like that as a paperweight. The decorated cookie from Germany would go in his little brother's stocking. The bell from America—that would be for his mother. Yes, Christmas was right here, it was the love in his heart.

The next morning was busy with gifts, then visits with friends, and finally the dinner at the manor house. With amazement he noticed that the usually mean manor house dog was sharing the big roast beef bones with Goliath.

When the feast was over, there was the sudden sound of trumpets. Lord Filbert stepped forward to make an important announcement. "I have worked out a plan so that those who are leasing land from me can now buy parcels and pay for them a little at a time. This will mean a better economy for the entire village but will still provide me with needed income. And so Lady Filbert and I wish a merry Christmas and the happiest of new years to you all!" Everyone cheered.

After the excitement of the announcement had died down, Lucia and David were asked to distribute candles to each person. Then the great chandeliers were turned off, and the many candles were lit— looking like hundreds of small stars. The party ended with everyone from the village joining Lord and Lady Filbert in singing "Silent Night" in the soft candlelight.

(SONG: "Silent Night")

At the end of the song, all was quiet. David saw that even Goliath was quiet—asleep by the fire, probably dreaming of his bone. The quiet reminded David of that night so long ago when Jesus was born—the beginning of this legend of love. His search for the real Christmas had ended.

Around the World for Christmas

"Hurrah for the Pudding!" From Little Folks, c. *1870*.

Chapter Six

Around the World for Christmas

Traditions, Feasts, and Recipes from Fourteen Countries

Many of the most memorable activities of Christmas come from around the world. We can enrich our own Christmas by learning more about how Christmas is celebrated in other countries. Perhaps you'll want to adopt a new tradition for your celebration, a new food for your feast, or a new way of saying "Merry Christmas" in another language.

So let's go on a world tour!

England

In a two-story brick house on the outskirts of London, the Smythe family is preparing for Christmas. Much has changed since the days of Charles Dickens, who, according to some jesters, actually "invented" Christmas with his detailed stories of the holiday season.

Some days ago George and Carolyn Smythe hung their stockings at the foot of their beds in the hope that Father Christmas would fill them with toys. It is an English tradition to write Father Christmas a letter, listing the hoped-for gifts. The letter is then tossed into the back of the fireplace, and if carried up the chimney, the wishes will be granted. But just to be sure, both George and Carolyn have also given a list to their parents.

Christmas in England is a merry time, with much pageantry, caroling, and feasting. In the Smythe living room there will be the wassail bowl, filled with a ceremonial Christmas drink. The word *wassail* comes from Old English and means "Be thou well." Originally, the wassail drink consisted of a mixture of ale, sugar, spices, eggs, and roasted apple, with thick cream added just before serving. In olden times, pieces of toast were floated on top, hence the origin of "drinking a toast."

In the Smythe living room, there will be a more modern wassail bowl. The immense pewter bowl that has been in the family for generations will hold mulled hot punch, and there will also be trays of pastries for guests. The Smythes are expecting relatives from the country for the Christmas Day feast.

Just a week ago, George and Carolyn made a trip into the city, and that day was almost as exciting as Christmas Day itself. Seeing the glittering lights on Regent Street, going to a hotel for high tea, hearing the chimes of Big Ben, riding a red double-decker bus to Trafalger Square to see the large lighted tree, hearing the caroling at the Tower of London—these were things their parents and grandparents had done before them, and though the children didn't consciously think about it, this trip was a link to the ceremonial past of England.

Now, on Christmas Eve, Carolyn sits by the fireplace, where the yule log burns brightly. When her father lit the log, using a piece of last year's log as kindling, he said the traditional prayer: "May the fire of this log warm the cold. May the hungry be fed. May the weary find rest, and may all enjoy heaven's peace."

Although most gifts will be opened on Christmas morning, the first weekday after Christmas is also an important gift-giving holiday. It is called Boxing Day, and the Smythes will join others in giving boxes of food, gifts, and money to their tradespeople and employees.

Boxing Day is also a day for sports and dances, and this year, because he is twelve, George will be taken by his uncle to his first fox hunt. So George is truly excited about both Christmas, when he'll be with his cousins, and the special events of Boxing Day.

At last the relatives arrive, and Mrs. Smythe has prepared a feast. While it does not include the old-fashioned boar's head, it does feature turkey with chestnut stuffing. The crowning touch to the meal is plum pudding, decorated with holly and brought to the table with a halo of flaming brandy.

Mrs. Smythe's Plum Pudding

Ingredients

1 cup flour
1 teaspoon salt
1 teaspoon baking soda
½ teaspoon nutmeg
1 teaspoon cinnamon
1½ cups chopped raisins
   (½ pound)
2 cups currants (½ pound)
1 cup finely chopped citron
   (¼ pound)
½ cup candied orange peel
¼ cup candied lemon peel

2 cups ground suet (½ pound)
   —obtainable from your
   butcher or meat department
1½ cups soft bread crumbs
¾ cup finely chopped walnuts
1 cup firmly packed brown
   sugar
3 eggs, beaten
⅓ cup currant jelly
¼ cup orange juice
Hard sauce (recipe follows)

Method:

Grease a ring or bowl-style mold. Place flour, salt, soda, cinnamon, and nutmeg in a large bowl and stir in bread crumbs, fruits, and nuts. Mix in a separate bowl the suet, brown sugar, eggs, jelly, and juice. Stir into first mixture. Pour into the mold and cover with aluminum foil. Put a rack into a Dutch oven and add boiling water to the level of the rack. Place mold on rack and cover the Dutch oven. Keep the water boiling over low heat to steam the pudding for four hours or until a toothpick comes out clean. (You may have to add water during this time. If so, add already boiling water.) Unmold, cut into slices, and serve warm with hard sauce.

Hard Sauce:

Ingredients:

½ cup butter or margarine
1 cup powdered sugar

2 teaspoons vanilla

Method:

Mix together ingredients and chill at least one hour before using.

Carolyn can't wait until the plum pudding is served. She especially loves the hard sauce—in fact her mother says, "Wouldn't you like a little plum pudding under your hard sauce?"

Along with mince tarts and the Christmas cake, first tasted on Christmas afternoon, there will be many other sweets. It is a tradition that you will have as many good months in the new year as tarts that you eat. George always manages to eat at least twelve!

One highlight of Christmas afternoon is the speech by the queen. Mr. Smythe tells how his parents and grandparents used to gather around the radio to hear the king. Now, the family and friends will see the queen give her message on live television.

At last it is time to open the gifts, and Carolyn, George, and their cousins hope that the tradition of throwing their lists into the fire really works. And it does! Now George hopes that the mincemeat tart tradition works just as well.

Holland

Hans doesn't wear wooden shoes as his ancestors did, but he does have a big pair that he uses every Christmas. Hans will place his wooden shoes on the hearth. He'll put hay and a carrot in one shoe for St. Nicholas's horse, and cookies and candy in the other for the old man himself.

Because the weather is dark, cold, and wet at Christmastime in Holland, December is called St. Nicholas weather. Other than ice and snow sports, most activities are indoors.

In Holland, there are many churches named for the legendary St. Nicholas, but on his special days, December 5th and 6th (St. Nicholas Eve and Day), the celebrations are not religious, but social. Hans and his family attend parties, exchange gifts, and feast on sweets.

Hans helps his mother make Janhagel, an easy-to-make almond cookie. He slices the almonds and tries not to eat too many of them.

Hans's Almond Crisps

Ingredients:

2 cups flour
¾ cup sugar
¼ teaspoon allspice
1½ teaspoons cinnamon

¾ cup butter
1 egg white
1½ cups sliced unblanched
  almonds

Method:

Combine first four ingredients in a large bowl. Cream the butter in a mixing bowl; then add the dry ingredients and mix well. Gradually add cold water, one teaspoon at a time, until mixture begins to hold together and forms a ball.

Roll out the dough between two pieces of waxed paper to a size that will fit a jelly roll pan or other baking pan. Grease and flour the baking pan. Then remove one of the waxed papers and turn the dough into the pan. Use your fingers to mend tears or to make the dough fit the pan. Beat the egg white with a tablespoon of water and brush dough with the mixture, then sprinkle almonds on top. Press almonds firmly into dough. Cut dough into bite-sized strips (about 1" x 2"). Bake in 350 degree oven for 20 to 25 minutes until dough is golden and almonds are browned. Let cookies stand about 5 minutes, then recut the lines made earlier. Remove from pan to a rack until cool.

These are the cookies Hans will leave for Sinterklaas (as St. Nicholas is often called) and his faithful friend, Black Peter. (Black Peter was originally symbolic of the devil, but today is a jolly joker who assists in present giving.) Little children believe that these two characters walk the roofs before December 5, listening at the chimneys to see if the family is deserving of gifts.

The official arrival of Sinterklaas and Black Peter takes place in Amsterdam harbor, where there are bands, church bells ringing, and a parade led by Sinterklaas and Black Peter to the royal palace. Here the monarch, or a representative, gives a report on the obedience of royal children, complete with their promises to be better.

In homes and businesses, St. Nicholas Eve and Day are times for gift giving. But there are two requirements: gifts must be accompanied by rhymes, and the gift must be disguised, not traditionally wrapped. So small gifts are stuffed into sausages or cauliflowers, and large gifts are hidden in the cellar or inside a box of rubbish. Adults especially enjoy the hiding of gifts, while children sometimes become impatient with the delay it causes.

As Christmas nears, the greeting "Blijde Kerstdagen" is heard everywhere in businesses and homes.

Christmas Eve and Christmas Day are celebrated much like Thanksgiving is in North America. There is a decorated tree, a large feast, church services, carols, and concerts—but no gifts, since they have already been given on St. Nicholas Day. However, in recent years, additional gifts have been given on Christmas morning.

Hans thinks that celebrating twice during the month is a wonderful tradition!

Spain

A Spanish Christmas can be a snowbound one if you live in the northern Catalonia region. Or it can be sun-drenched if you live in the province of Cadiz. Either way, Christmas is primarily a religious holiday in Spain.

Carlos lives with his grandparents in Barcelona, where Christmas is bright and sunny. His favorite decoration is the *nacimiento*—the nativity scene. The one at his house was made generations ago and is surrounded by many candles. To the family, it is more important than a Christmas tree.

The Virgin Mary is the patron saint of Spain, and December 8 is set aside as a day to honor her. (For Catholics everywhere, December 8 is celebrated as a Marian feast.) Houses are decorated with flowers, flags, and candles, and in Seville's great cathedral a ceremony called *Los Seises* ("Dance of the Six") takes place. Over the years the number of dancers has grown, and today it is performed with ten boys dressed in baroque costumes of blue satin with plumed hats.

This year, Carlos was chosen as one of the dancers, and with the others was trained under ecclesiastical direction. Then, on December 8, they traveled by bus to the cathedral. Carlos had never been this far from home!

The dance was performed just after vespers with candles giving the chapel a golden hue. The dance movements of line, star, double chain or wheel all have deep religious meanings—and the dancers did them perfectly. Carlos felt honored to have been chosen.

Now he is looking forward to the Christmas service in the great cathedral, but he shyly admits that he also likes to dance in the square with his friends. After midnight mass on Christmas Eve, everyone gathers in the streets to sing carols and dance to the tinkling of tambourines, gourds, and castanets. Carlos doesn't worry about getting lost in the huge crowd because his grandparents enjoy the dancing just as much as he does, and they will be nearby.

The scene at the great cathedral is one Carlos never tires of. As they walk up the stairs, they look at all the booths where *nacimiento* figures are sold, as well as wreaths and other decorations. Inside, many

choirs take their turns singing. And everywhere there are candles and more candles.

Because Christmas Day will be reserved for family and relatives, Christmas Eve is the time when homes are lighted in welcome for the visits of friends. For sure there will be lots of a special nougat candy that Carlos loves to eat. It is called *turron* and is sold in markets everywhere, even from door to door. The rich and poor alike eat it throughout the holidays.

There will also be traditional festive foods made by his grandmother—one being a most impressive dish with three names: Olla-Podrida, Puchero, or Cocido. Because it cooks all afternoon, it gives the house a wonderful aroma. It is given here under its ancient name.

Olla-Podrida

Ingredients:

1 pound beef brisket	1 onion
¼ pound lamb shoulder	1 cabbage
¼ pound ham in chunks	¼ pound chick-peas
¼ pound salt pork in thick pieces	(garbanzos) well-soaked
1 split breast of chicken	4 large garlic cloves
2 chorizos (Spanish sausages)	4 potatoes
2 carrots	Seasonings

Method:

Put all the meat except chicken and sausage in a large pot and cover with cold water. Bring to a boil, remove any scum, and add crushed garlic and the soaked chick-peas. Cover and cook gently for 2 hours. Add chicken and sausage. Slice vegetables in chunks and add all but the potatoes. Cook for 1 hour more. Add salt and pepper to taste, then add the potatoes. Simmer for 45 minutes more. As cooking proceeds, take out the meats that are done, as some will require less time. Arrange all the meats on a platter. Serve the soup from a tureen.

Carlos thinks that this dish tastes as wonderful as it smells. Besides, it means that it is Christmas Eve, and that means he will receive one gift. But his other gifts must wait for Epiphany (twelve days after Christmas).

Carlos knows the old legend that each year the wise men travel through Spain en route to Bethlehem. Out on the roads leading into the city, the children—carrying cakes and candy—await the wise men on the eve of Epiphany. Somehow they never see the magi, and thus they cannot bestow their food gifts. It is later reported that the wise men entered and left the city by other routes. However, when the children return home they find a gift left for them by the magi—and they then consume all the special cakes and candy themselves!

With his grandparents, Carlos makes his way home through the city square. He is sleepy but excited about the gift that will be waiting at home. With the others he shouts, "Felices Pascuas."

Sweden

The Jacobson house in Gothenburg is usually a noisy one, but on the morning of December 13, there are only whispers. Berit and Kerstin, along with their brothers, Gunnar and Erik, are preparing for Santa Lucia Day. Prior to this morning, cardamom cakes, cinnamon buns, Lussekatter (special Lucia buns), and pepparkakor (ginger cookies) have all been made.

The Santa Lucia tradition, which marks the beginning of the Swedish month-long celebration, originally came from Sicily. Lucia, known as the Queen of Light, was born in Sicily, where she served the poor and imprisoned, bringing light into their dark lives. On the eve of her marriage, she gave away her entire dowry to the poor and proclaimed she had become a Christian. Accused of witchcraft, she died a martyr's death on December 13, A.D. 304. Many years later she was made a saint.

Then, folklore has it that during a famine in medieval times, she brought much-needed food to Sweden. In the cold dark days near the time of the winter solstice, she became a symbol of hope and charity, and the Swedish people have celebrated her coming ever since.

In the towns and cities of Sweden, Santa Lucias are chosen from among the local girls, and pageants honoring her are held. Because the tradition is that Lucia was dressed in white with a luminous halo, the girls nowadays dress in white gowns with silver trim and wear a wreath with candles on their heads.

In each home, the tradition continues with Santa Lucia (the oldest daughter) bringing breakfast to family members. Since Berit is the oldest daughter, she will lead the processional at her house. She will wear a long white gown—actually a nightgown—and a wreath of tinsel in her hair. Carrying the tray of foods and coffee, she will sing the Italian song "Santa Lucia" and awaken her parents. So begins Christmas for the Jacobsons.

But Berit's little sister, Kerstin, is far more excited about Jultomten, the elf responsible for bringing gifts on Christmas Eve. And when that day finally comes all the children dress in their most festive clothing for a celebration that lasts about twelve hours.

Businesses close, and everyone gathers in homes, in the kitchen where candles and vases of flowers and pine branches decorate the room. Here the traditional dipping of bread in the pot, known as *doppa i grytan*, takes place. Dark bread is speared on forks and dipped in a mixture of pork, corned beef, and sausage drippings in commemoration of the ancient famine when the only food was dark bread and broth. When this ritual is over, the celebration begins.

Although many homes now have less elaborate meals, the Jacobsons observe the traditional smorgasbord and dinner, because they have a large family and any extra food can be used the next day.

The smorgasbord consists of limpa bread, butter, cheeses, herrings, red beets, pickled cucumber, patés and meatballs. Then comes the traditional meal with *lutfisk* (sun-cured cod, served with a cream sauce), boiled potatoes, ham, red cabbage, and other hearty foods.

Christmas songs are often sung before the *aquavit* (a strong alcoholic drink) is served and the family moves to the living room.

Dessert consists of rice pudding (rice cooked in cream with cinnamon) and trays of cookies and pastries. Cooked into the pudding is one almond, and the person finding it will supposedly marry within the year. Everyone laughs when Erik finds the nut, since he is only seven years old.

Now comes the time that Kerstin and the other children have waited for: the giving of gifts. There is no hurry in opening them—in fact, the children won't go to bed until after midnight. And they can sleep late the next morning, since there will be no rush to see what is under the Christmas tree, because the gifts will have been opened already.

Some families continue the tradition of attending church in the early hours of Christmas morn. In olden times it was the custom to race home from the service in sleds or horse-drawn wagons. The winner was predicted to have the best harvest in the coming year.

But Christmas Day is busy with visits to relatives and more eating. Gunnar likes to look at the ornaments on all the trees: straw goats and other animals, strings of Swedish flags, and stars.

At their aunt's house, they have another feast, which includes this traditional dish.

Jansson's Frestelse (Mr. Jansson's Temptation)

Ingredients:

14-16 anchovies
2 large yellow onions
8-10 boiling potatoes
1½ cups whipping cream

2 tablespoons butter or margarine
Bread crumbs and additional butter for topping

Method:

Peel potatoes and cut into thin strips. Peel and thinly slice onions. Brown onions and potatoes in the butter. Alternate layers of potatoes and onions with the anchovies, ending with a potato layer. Pour the cream over the dish, sprinkle with bread crumbs, and dot with butter. Bake at 400 degrees until potatoes are soft—45 to 60 minutes.

After this meal, the family receives a customary marzipan confection in the shape of a large pig. Back home, this pig (called a *Julgrisen*) is placed on the coffee table in the living room, and the children eat it by breaking off pieces over the course of the next few days.

The following day, December 26, is one of Berit's favorites. It is Saint Stephen's Day, which commemorates the patron saint of animals. Farm animals get extra rations, but at Berit's home the honoree is her beloved dog, who feasts on some leftovers from the Christmas Eve smorgasbord.

The next holiday is Twelfth Night, the night that celebrates the arrival of the wise men in Bethlehem. Children dress in costumes, usually those of biblical characters, and walk through the city carrying poles topped with paper stars with candles inside them. They sing hymns and songs about the wise men as they stroll along.

One week later, Christmas finally comes to an end on January 13— one month from Santa Lucia Day. This holiday is called *Knut*. The tree is lighted for the last time, and as the children help extinguish the candles, Berit is already thinking ahead eleven months when it will all start again.

Switzerland

Heidi and Jacques Meyer have the best of two cultures. Their mother is from the French part of Switzerland and their father from the German part. So their family traditions follow those of two different cultures.

The Meyer home, high on a hill outside Zurich, is in traditional chalet style, but inside it is very up-to-date. Still, Mr. Meyer insists on having a Christmas tree with candles rather than electric lights. Most residential trees will have candles, but the trees in stores and in the village square have electric lights. Heidi loves to decorate their tree with colored glass balls, gold garlands, and angels. Jacques helps to add the final touch: chocolates! He tries hard not to eat too many as he decorates the tree.

The children's celebration at church will be held during the week before Christmas. Along with the worship service, they will sing in both French and German—"Douce Nuit" and "Stille Nacht." Jacques can also sing this song as "Silent Night" in English. His next favorite song is called "Minuit Chrétien." At the end of the program, each participant will receive a special cookie with sugar decoration. Also that week, the family will go to a concert that will include the singing of Handel's *Messiah*.

The Christmas Eve celebration will include a feast of *Canard à l'orange* (Duck with orange sauce) and all the trimmings. The finale will be a family recipe for a special pudding called a mousse.

Mousse au Chocolat

Ingredients:

4 eggs, separated
½ pound sweet chocolate

1 heaping tablespoon butter
Whipped cream

Method:

Melt chocolate over low heat and add egg yolks and butter. Stir well. Beat egg whites until very stiff and fold into chocolate mixture. Put in six small dishes and refrigerate. Top with whipped cream before serving.

The Meyers have wisely decided that gift-giving is getting out of hand, so this year, there will be just the most wanted toys. Jacques is hoping for an electronic toy or a computer game cassette, while Heidi wants the traditional wooden toys—cars, houses, people, animals, a train.

In their fireplace is the yule log and on the front door is a wreath-style decoration called the crown of advent. Outside, as Heidi and Jacques play in the snow, every direction they turn looks like a Christmas card scene of mountains and trees and tiny villages.

As Heidi and Jacques are making a snow man, neighbors pass by. They can shout in French, "Joyeux Noël!" or in German, "Frohe Weihnachten!"

Italy

Donna is thinking about Christmas Eve. It is a day of fasting—there will be no food until the end of the day. But she doesn't mind at all, because the feast will more than make up for the fast.

At sundown the Mastrantonio family will gather around the *Presepio*—the beloved nativity scene with its little figures of shepherds, wise men, Joseph, and Mary. The family prays together, and then Donna's mother will place the final figure in the scene: the bambino. With the addition of the infant Jesus, the scene is complete. Then Christmas gifts are distributed!

While some families do not eat until the next day, Donna's family observes the modern custom of a large feast before the midnight mass. Tortellini (pasta filled with meat), fried eels, and panettone (a delicious bread) will be among the many foods served. Afterward, there will be trays of sweets.

Donna helps make the panettone. Here is a simple version of this special bread.

Panettone

Ingredients:

3¾ cups flour
½ cup butter, softened
½ cup brown sugar
3 eggs
4 egg yolks
⅔ ounce yeast
3 teaspoons salt

2 tablespoons powdered sugar
2 additional tablespoons
   powdered sugar
¼ cup sultana raisins
¼ cup candied citron
   peel, diced
¼ cup granulated sugar

Method:

Put the flour in a large bowl and make a well in the middle. Into the well add the salt, the whole eggs, brown sugar diluted in 2 tablespoons of water, 5 tablespoons of the butter, and the yeast. Mix these ingredients in the well. Then, incorporate the flour, a little at a time. Next, stir the dough vigorously until it does not stick to your hands. Turn it out on a wooden board and spread into a layer about ¾" thick. Sprinkle with 2 tablespoons of powdered sugar. Add 2 of the egg yolks and the remaining butter softened into a paste. Scatter raisins and citron on top and blend while kneading dough for a few minutes. Roll into a ball, put in a buttered and floured baking pan and set aside in a warm place to allow the dough to rise until doubled in size. Turn into baking pan. Then make a mixture of the 2 remaining egg yolks diluted with 2 teaspoons of water, a pinch of flour, and 2 tablespoons of powdered sugar. Brush the top with the mixture. With a sharp knife, make several incisions in the top of the loaf. Sprinkle with granulated sugar. Bake at 375 degrees for 50-60 minutes.

As exciting as Christmas Day is, the real celebration comes at Epiphany (the celebration of the magi twelve days after Christmas) with the arrival of a female version of Saint Nicholas, called La Befana. Befana brings gifts to good children and sticks or switches to bad ones. Donna likes the tradition, for she knows it is just a myth—and besides, she is usually a good girl.

A favorite tradition of Donna's is not observed often nowadays. It is called the *pifferari*. Ten days before the end of Advent, shepherds dressed in sheepskin trousers, bright red vests, and broad-brimmed hats with red tassels and white peacock feathers march into the towns from the outlying districts. They carry bagpipes, reeds, and oboes and play music before each shrine of the Holy Child. They pause before carpenter shops in honor of Joseph. At some homes, like Donna's, they will be invited inside to sing old carols and folk songs.

As they depart, there are the shouts of Merry Christmas in the air: "Buon Natale!"

Germany

There is a small Christmas tree for each person at Ingrid's house. While many families have not continued this old custom, the Hahn family has. Their home has all the traditional decorations, including the pyramidal candlestand called a "lightstock," which commemorates Jesus as the light of the world.

The Hahns have a wood-carved nativity scene that has been in the family for two centuries. Though the paint has faded, Ingrid still enjoys holding each piece and looking at the deftly carved faces and the clothing—so lifelike that it looks like fabric rather than wood. In the Hahn home are many decorations as well as traditions originating in Germany that have traveled around the world.

Ingrid's older brother, Wilhelm, has an important part in the church service this year. He will be one of the "cradle rockers." Folklore customs require that the Christchild be given as many creature comforts as possible. And so, there is in many churches a cradle with an effigy of a baby in it. As the carols are sung, the altar boys take turns rocking the cradle. Wilhelm will try to remember to rock the cradle gently, not wildly as he did when Ingrid was a baby and he almost tossed her out over the side of the family cradle.

Mr. Hahn has already hung the wreath of greens, with its four candles, from a beam in the sitting room. One candle will be lighted on each Sunday of Advent (the four weeks before Christmas).

Mrs. Hahn will roast a goose and make her husband's special torte, which will be eaten Christmas Eve.

Blitz Torte

Ingredients:

¾ cup butter
¾ cup sugar
4 egg yolks
1 cup flour
1 teaspoon baking powder
2 teaspoons vanilla

5 tablespoons milk
4 egg whites
1 additional cup of sugar
2 ounces slivered blanched
   almonds
Filling (recipe below)

Method:

With an electric mixer, cream butter, then add sugar and cream the mixture again. Add egg yolks one at a time, beating slowly. Add flour and baking powder at lowest speed, then add vanilla and milk. Spread dough in two 9" layer cake pans. Beat 4 egg whites until stiff, adding one cup of sugar, beating again until very stiff. Spread over dough. Sprinkle almonds on top. Bake at 350 degrees for 20 minutes.

Filling:

1½ cups sour cream
2 tablespoons sugar
1 tablespoon cornstarch

1 whole egg
1 tablespoon vanilla

Method:

Boil together until stiff, add vanilla when cool. Spread between the two layers of cooled cake. Refrigerate until ready to serve.

Ingrid loves to walk through their town. Most stores cater to the children with magical displays of toys and games, many of them hand-made and quite expensive. She has seen a string puppet that she would love to have. If Wilhelm got one, too, they could put on plays together.

On Christmas Eve, the tree will be lighted for the first time, and they will all exchange gifts. She can hardly wait!

Ingrid says Merry Christmas this way: "Froehliche Weihnachten."

Eastern Europe

Through the years, Ana's family has celebrated Christmas in several different countries—but always in the same house! Because of many border changes, the Smetana family has had to adjust to new rulers; however, Christmas has remained much the same through many generations. Ana's family celebration brings together Hungarian, Czechoslovakian, and Russian traditions, rich in beauty and meaning.

Ana's grandmother Marya had been accustomed to celebrating Christmas by the Julian calendar—which made it January 7—and when Ana was little there were two celebrations. But this became too expensive, and Marya agreed to the December date as long as the family "kept Christmas" in the old tradition.

Because the celebration of Christ's birth is the foremost part of the holiday, Ana always wears a special outfit purchased just for the churchgoing occasions. Adults attend midnight mass, and children go on Christmas morning. Since gifts are opened on Christmas Eve, there is no problem doing both.

Ana has been taught to perform at least one good deed during Advent. This year she has chosen to shovel a neighbor's sidewalk each time it snows. This has been hard work, but she has done it with grace, and she enjoys the smiles and thank-you hugs she receives. She is aware that her brother Mikail has chosen something easier. He will donate a toy for a child who must spend Christmas in the hospital.

The Christmas focus at the Smetana house is the Christmas tree. Ana and Mikail play around it, have quiet times reading stories under it, and gather around it before bed to say their prayers and admire its beauty. The children make one new ornament for the tree each year. The emphasis is always on something found in nature, something that would please the baby Jesus. So this year they attach pretty ribbons to a pine cone Ana found and a tiny bird nest that Mikail found abandoned.

Their big old house is decorated with a candle in every window and a special candle on the table, which has been blessed at church and is lit just for the Christmas Eve meal. When it is extinguished, everyone watches the way the smoke goes. If it goes upward, it signifies a prosperous year ahead. There is straw under the tablecloth to signify the manger. It makes a few lumps, but that makes eating more fun. And, at the end of each meal, a carol is sung.

The biggest gathering of young cousins and other relatives is on Christmas Eve. When everyone has arrived, they all gather in the kitchen and listen for the arrival of St. Nicholas. Suddenly there is the sound of jingling bells. The children are transfixed and don't want to spoil the magic by rushing into the living room. When the front door slams shut, they race to see what St. Nicholas has brought, unaware that one of the uncles has been absent during this time.

This year, Ana's favorite gifts are a handmade sweater and a matching one for her doll. Mikail likes the wooden toys, and, with his cousin, he immediately takes over the living room floor. Adults exclaim over paperweights and picture frames and original poems.

But the feast is still to come. During the day there is fasting: water, crackers, fruit, and toast are all that is eaten. And, at the feast, which is a modified fast, no animal product is served. This is to honor the holy family who had little to eat on their long journey to Bethlehem. And in the manger they shared quarters with the friendly beasts, rather than eating them.

Because Grandma and Grandpa grew up in a tradition-filled Carpathian village, the custom continues to serve twelve foods, none derived from an animal. These were in honor of the twelve apostles and included unleavened bread, honey, cloves of garlic (which were baked into the bread, and those getting one would be assured of a particularly healthy year), small crisp potatoes, peas mashed with garlic, white beans, mushrooms, sweet and sour cabbage, plums, oil, onions, and *pirohi* (dumplings).

But Ana could hardly wait for dessert, a special pastry treat made by her mamma.

Kolachki
(pronounced Ko-lotch-key)

Ingredients:

1 pound cream cheese (2 large packages), softened
4½ cups all-purpose flour
1 pound margarine or butter, softened

2 egg whites
Nut Filling (recipe below)

Method:

Cream the softened margarine and cream cheese together. Slowly mix in the flour until the mixture is a soft dough. Wrap in foil and chill overnight. The next day, take small sections of the dough and roll it out. (Be sure to keep the remaining dough well-chilled.) Cut it into strips 1½" x 2". Fill one end with a small amount of the nut filling and roll pastry to form a mini-roll. Seal the edge with the egg white. Bake on an ungreased cookie sheet for 10 to 15 minutes in a preheated 400 degree oven. They should be light brown—beware of burning them. Cool, pack in an airtight tin, and keep cool until serving. Just before serving, sprinkle with powdered sugar.

Nut Filling:

1 pound whole shelled walnuts
2 cups granulated sugar

Water

Method:

Grind nuts finely. Add sugar. Add water until mixture forms a stiff paste.

Ana and Mikail look forward to staying up late on Christmas Eve. When the adults return from midnight mass, there will be treats for everyone—hot chocolate and kolachki.

These are the words Ana uses to wish you a Merry Christmas:

ХРИСТОС РАЖДАЕТША

Tasmania

For Karen and John, fresh raspberries mark the coming of Christmas. In Tasmania, it is summertime in December, and their father's business is growing the luscious berries. The school holiday starts in mid-December and goes until mid-February, so many families celebrate Christmas and then go on vacation to the beaches.

Karen and John also know that the Christmas season has started when the television plays carols each night before the news program. And this year they got to see a Santa when they were in the city shopping with their mother. On city street corners everywhere and in many neighborhoods, the Salvation Army sings carols.

This year John helped his father pack a hamper for a needy family. They shared raspberries they had grown and milk from their dairy cows. Karen and her mother made sweaters for each member of the family.

Special foods mark the holiday meal. Karen's favorite is crayfish. John's favorite is the Christmas pudding. He likes it so much that he always offers to mix the ingredients together.

John's Frozen Christmas Pudding

Ingredients:

1 liter of vanilla ice cream
1 cup of mixed fruit (John
   likes to include raspberries)
½ cup chopped mixed nuts

½ cup glazed cherries
½ cup port (cherry, berry, or
   peach juice can be substituted)
½ cup cream

Method:

Soften ice cream in a large bowl. Add all other ingredients and mix together. Refreeze.

While most Tasmanian Christmas traditions are similar to those in England and the United States, some of the decorations for the Christmas tree are rather unique. Karen and John especially like the toy koala bears tucked into little stockings!

Asia

Kung lives in China, where Christmas has been celebrated for only half a century. But with less than 1 percent of the population practicing Christians, the country-wide celebration will be modest. Kung calls Christmas the Holy Birth Festival, and the Christmas tree is called the Tree of Light.

Kung hangs his Christmas stocking in the hope that Nice Old Father, the name for the Santa figure, will fill it with gifts. His tree is bright with color and glitter. Flowers and chains made of paper and cut-outs of butterflies and temples trim the tree. Tiny lanterns cover the lights on the tree and give it an oriental distinction.

Kung thinks that the best part—aside from the gifts—is the fireworks that are used to usher in the holiday. It is also a time for great feasts and parades with jugglers and acrobats.

In Japan, the birthday of the Christchild has been celebrated for only about one hundred years. Mari and her parents have adopted many of the Western customs, including exchanging gifts, eating turkey, decorating with mistletoe and holly, and having the traditional decorations on the tree.

While Mari is too old to believe the Santa myth, she laughs with the older children at the *Hoteiosho*—one of their gods, who also serves as Santa Claus for the children. The tradition is that this kind old man has eyes in the back of his head so he can watch the behavior of the children and decide if they should receive gifts.

Many ornaments sold around the world are manufactured in Japan. In fact, Mari's father's business designs tassels and trims for clothing as well as for ornaments. With the leftovers from the manufacture of these, Mari has decorated their tree.

Although very few Japanese are Christians, many non-Christians enjoy the bustle of Christmas shopping and partying. However, the leading holiday is the New Year's celebration—a three-day event with street decorations, pine branches at the entrance gates of homes, visiting, kite-flying, gift-giving, and parades. Toys are used to decorate the tree branches and are later given to the children.

Mari loves to bake these cookies for her family and friends.

Snappy Lemon Snaps

Ingredients:

2 lemons
1 cup sugar
2 cups flour
2 teaspoons baking powder
½ teaspoon baking soda

¼ teaspoon ground ginger
½ cup butter or margarine
1 egg
2 teaspoons light corn syrup
1 teaspoon lemon juice

Method:

With a sharp knife, peeler, or zester, remove the thin outer layer from the lemons. Using a food processor, combine this lemon zest with the sugar. (Use the steel blade for 2-3 minutes.) Then strain to remove any large pieces of lemon peel. Set aside 2 tablespoons of this lemon-sugar for the topping.

Mix the flour, baking powder and soda, and ginger in a bowl. With an electric mixer, combine and beat the butter and 1 cup of the lemon-sugar mixture. Add the egg, syrup, and lemon juice and beat until smooth. Then gradually add the dry ingredients.

Form the dough into balls and place on greased baking pans about 2" apart. Sprinkle very lightly with the lemon-sugar mixture and press balls flat, using the bottom of a greased glass.

Bake at 375 degrees for 8 to 10 minutes until cookies are just slightly dark around the edges. After removing from the oven, let cookies remain on the pan for a few minutes, then remove to a rack until completely cooled.

Hawaii

The day for Santa's arrival has finally come. Kalani and Ginger ride their bikes down the hill from their home in Makiki and through Waikiki to the shoreline. Tourists and locals crowd the water's edge for this exciting event.

Out where the waves are breaking, they see the familiar figure in the red suit. Suddenly, Santa catches a wave and deftly rides his surfboard all the way into the sandy beach. Christmas has come to Hawaii!

The Christmas that Kalani and Ginger will celebrate in Hawaii is similar to that in other states of the United States, but there are some unique features. Without snow, Santa comes by surfboard. Santas on street corners collecting for charity say that they swelter inside their heavy suits.

Christmas trees suffer the most from the weather. They are shipped from the mainland by boat and so in order to arrive on time, they are cut in early autumn, which often results in a dried out tree. Kalani and Ginger's family have a remedy for that. They buy a tree and have it flocked. The flocking helps "glue" the needles in place for the holiday season and also introduces a feeling of snow into their living room. Still, a Christmas with warm weather can include Christmas day swims and walks in the sun.

On Christmas Eve, they will go to the historic Kawaiahao Church to sing carols in both English and Hawaiian.

But today Kalani and Ginger are excitedly talking about all the coming events. They walk their bikes back home again, talking about the school program where they'll sing all the familiar Christmas songs.

Back in their house, they decide to make *Maia Hoomo'a*, one of their favorite banana dishes. Out in the yard, they pull down a big hand of bananas and find just enough ripe ones for their lunch.

Kalani's Baked Bananas

Ingredients:

6 ripe bananas   Butter, salt, and pepper to taste

Method:

Wash the bananas. Do not peel them. Place them in a baking pan with just enough water to cover the bottom of the pan. Bake at 350 degrees for 30 to 45 minutes until the bananas are soft and the skins begin to pop open. Serve hot in the skins with butter, salt, and pepper.

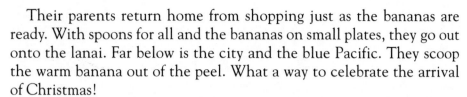

Their parents return home from shopping just as the bananas are ready. With spoons for all and the bananas on small plates, they go out onto the lanai. Far below is the city and the blue Pacific. They scoop the warm banana out of the peel. What a way to celebrate the arrival of Christmas!

It is time once more for "Mele Kalikimaka"—a merry Christmas-time in the islands of Hawaii.

Mexico

Rosa, Marcos, and Carmela live in Oaxaca, where one of the biggest Mexican Christmas markets is held. While they will not spend money there, they will look at all the toys and decorations with their parents.

Christmas in Mexico means posadas, piñatas, and puestos. The Contreras family will go to the less expensive puestos (Indian market stalls) to do most of their shopping. There they will find pottery, paintings, carvings, and woven items, as well as special cheeses, peppers, and sweets. The Contreras home is already bright with poinsettias outside, and inside the many candles in every room of the adobe are ready to be lighted.

It is nine days before Christmas and time for Las Posadas, the ceremony commemorating the trip of Mary and Joseph from Nazareth to Bethlehem. *Posada* means "inn" or "lodging place," and in many towns there is a procession in honor of the holy family's fruitless search for a place to lodge.

Rosa's family and friends always arrange several nights for posadas. They meet at one house, and the participants are divided into two groups—pilgrims and innkeepers. First there is a processional with candles around the outside of the house. Then, the innkeepers go into the house and take their positions in various rooms. Moving from room to room, the pilgrims ask for shelter, saying a special litany, and are refused admittance by the innkeepers. Finally when the pilgrims reach a room where an altar has been set up, this innkeeper invites them to enter. Here they find the nativity scene staged against a small simulated hillside of miniature homes and animals.

Often a piñata party follows the posada. The piñata is a large pottery or papier-mâché container in the shape of an animal or other object. It contains candy and small toys and is suspended from a branch or beam. Each child is blindfolded, whirled around several times, and then given a big stick for hitting the piñata. Sometimes it takes many hits to break apart the piñata. Finally there is a scramble for the goodies as they fall to the ground.

On Christmas Eve there will be a candlelight procession from the church to the plaza and then back to the church for midnight mass. Everyone carries lanterns attached to the end of a branch or wand, making a moving line of light.

When Rosa and her family come home after mass, they will not exchange gifts, but they will start the preparations for the Christmas Day feast. On Christmas Day they will light the luminarias along the path to their house to lead their friends to the door.

One special dish that will be served has olives in it—and Rosa loves olives!

Chicken with Olives

Ingredients:

3½ pound fryer chicken,
  cut into pieces
Salt and pepper to taste
2 tablespoons olive oil
1½ cups finely chopped
  onion
3 cloves garlic, minced
¼ cup dry sherry, divided

2 teaspoons chili powder
1 teaspoon cumin
1 teaspoon ground oregano
1 tablespoon flour
3 cups chopped tomatoes
  (or 18 oz. can peeled plum
  tomatoes, drained)
24 pitted green olives

Method:

Season chicken with salt and pepper. Heat the olive oil in a heavy skillet. Add the chicken, skin side down, and cook until brown; then turn and brown the other side. Place chicken pieces in a large pot with cover (like a Dutch oven). Add onion to skillet and stir and cook until limp. Add garlic and half of sherry and cook until most of the liquid has evaporated. Stir in chili powder, cumin, oregano, and flour and blend. Add tomatoes. Salt and pepper to taste. Cook until thickened, stirring often.

Spoon sauce over chicken. Cover and cook over moderate heat 30 minutes or until chicken is tender. Add olives and remaining sherry. Bring just to a boil. Remove from heat and serve with rice.

There will be all the traditional Mexican foods, but no gifts. The children must wait for these until January 6, a day honoring the arrival of the wise men. Even baby Carmela has been taught to say, "Feliz Navidad!"

The Holy Land

Kandra attends school just outside of Jerusalem. Her family are Christian Arabs, and they are accustomed to the difficulties of celebrating Christmas in the Jewish homeland.

Just the same, the customs of Christmas are important to her, and this year her school has been chosen as one of the many schools to sing at the site of the manger in Bethlehem. This is a great honor, and they have practiced their three songs over and over again.

But that won't happen until Christmas Eve. First, her family must prepare their own home for Christmas. Candles are an absolute essential, and since there is little money to spare, they make their own and decorate them with trimmings bought at the bazaar in Jerusalem.

Kandra loves to go to the bazaar with her mother. They follow the many winding streets looking for inexpensive decorations and special foods.

One day while her mother was bargaining for some fabric, Kandra went to the next stall and found the perfect gift for her parents—a small wood carving. It took all her money, but it pleased her to walk home with it hidden in her pocket. She ran her fingers over the smoothly carved olive wood—this would be a wonderful surprise.

With her mother, Kandra helps to make treats—ones that taste good, but are also beautiful.

The Cookie Ring

Ingredients:

1 cup butter, softened
2 egg yolks
1 teaspoon vanilla
2¼ cups flour

⅔ cup sugar
For decoration: red and
    green maraschino cherries,
    citron, and dates.

Method:

   Cream butter, gradually add sugar and cream again. Add egg yolks one at a time, continuing to beat. Add flavoring. Beat well while adding flour a little at a time, to form dough. On a floured board, roll out dough and cut into rounds of about 2½" diameter. On a large flat cookie sheet, place rounds to form a large circle, each cookie overlapping about ½ of the next cookie. Decorate with red and green maraschino cherries, citron, and dates. Bake at 350 degrees for about 20 minutes, until golden brown. Loosen from pan while hot. When cool, carefully slide onto serving tray.

   This year the family hopes to have a Christmas tree—a real luxury in Israel. It isn't that trees are so expensive, it is just that they are hard to find. In Israel, tree planting is very important, and tree cutting is frowned upon.

   But Kandra's family knows where trees will be available for one day only. Together they go in the old family car and arrive just in time to get one of the last small trees. It is like a treasure to them.

   That evening they trim it with homemade ornaments. Under it are placed the gifts, one for each family member. These will be opened after church on Christmas morning.

   When Christmas Eve comes, buses are ready to take the singers and their families to nearby Bethlehem. The new road makes it an easy trip, past the field of the shepherds and close to the city. For security reasons, no vehicles will be permitted inside Bethlehem, so they must leave the bus and walk the remainder of the way to Bethlehem Square and the Church of the Nativity.

Along with pilgrims, other Christians, and tourists, they have a lighthearted walk. But once inside the city, Kandra sees the many soldiers—at every street corner and on the tops of buildings. It is a scary sight at this season meant for commemorating love and peace. It is now eight o'clock, and they must be back on the buses by midnight.

There is so much to see. The square is decorated with small lights. The shops are all open, and tempting foods and gifts are offered. Only the tourists seem to be buying. But Kandra sees a small wool hat with bright stripes that would be perfect for cold days. It reminds her of Joseph's coat of many colors. But it costs too much money—and besides, it is time to go into the church.

As they make their way through the incense-filled chapels inside the church, she hears singing and chanting in many languages. The haze of incense makes it seem like a dream.

Finally she and her schoolmates reach the stone-sided room. Pilgrims are lined up to touch or kiss the large silver star set in the floor over the traditional place where Jesus was born. There is a little stone alcove off to one side, where Kandra's teacher lines them up to sing.

The visitors silently enter the cave-like room under the church. Most carry candles, and all are dressed warmly despite the stuffiness of the church. Many will remain for midnight services and the ringing of the bells. The visitors smile at the young singers. Kandra wonders what Christmas is like in their many different homelands. She thinks it must be more fun than here, where the tensions of violence and war make living difficult.

Now it is time to sing, and their voices blend in sweet harmony. When the children finish singing, their teacher leads them out of the church through a side door into a courtyard, where the Anglican church is holding a songfest. The priests with their black robes and tall mitred hats smile at the children and encourage them to stay and sing one song together. Kandra joins in the singing of "O Little Town of Bethlehem."

Her teacher whispers to them that this is a beloved carol written by an American preacher who visited Bethlehem in 1865. He wrote the words in a notebook as he walked in the fields outside the old city. She hears the words sung:

In thy dark streets shineth
The everlasting light;
The hopes and fears of all the years
Are met in thee tonight.

Outside in the square, she no longer fears the soldiers. The students gather for treats and then walk together past the shops. She wants to show her friend the special wool hat, but it is gone. Soon they must go to the meeting place where the parents will be waiting.

As the family walks back to the buses, she notices that her father is carrying a small brown-paper wrapped package. What could it be?

Along the way, they stop and look up at the clear sky. The stars shine and wink, and Kandra has a feeling of contentment.

It is midnight as they climb onto the bus. In the distance, the bells of Bethlehem begin to toll the arrival of Christmas Day. Kandra snuggles between her parents and falls asleep.

The Boy Who Hated Christmas

"Preparing Christmas Greens," by T. De Thulstrup. From Harper's Weekly, *Dec. 25, 1880.*

Chapter Seven

The Boy Who Hated Christmas

A Story for Teens

The Stanley High School bus rumbled to a stop at the corner of Collins Avenue. The first to get off was a boy who jumped down, quickly crossed to the opposite side of the street, and headed toward the sprawling frame house at the corner. Next off were two girls deep in conversation.

Years ago, Collins Avenue had been a wide and beautiful driveway for just one spacious home. Then, in the late 1920s, the property was divided, leaving the trees that formed a green arch over the street as a reminder of the elegant past. Now, in early December, they stood gray and bare in the winter sun. Through the years, the growing city surrounded Collins Avenue, so that, just a few blocks away, tall buildings poked up like a picket fence around this little oasis.

Arms loaded with books, the two girls tried to act oblivious to the tall, handsome boy with tousled dark hair. Actually they were quite interested in him.

"Why didn't you tell me that Tim Powell lived on your street?" demanded Sonja. "What's he like?"

"How should I know?" replied Donna. "He's lived here four months and doesn't even know I'm alive. Maybe he thinks seniors should ignore juniors. All he does is study, study, study. He even studies in study hall!"

Sonja laughed. "When the others get to your house, we'll have to ask about him. I'm sure Nguyen knows him—they're on the academic decathlon team together."

They let themselves into the Davis house, found the note and food left by Donna's mother, and proceeded to the basement, trays of soft drinks and brownies in hand.

"How many are coming—aside from us and Nguyen? We have a lot to do, and you and I will probably have to do most of the work," complained Sonja.

Donna counted on her fingers: "No way. Leslie, Barb, Will, Sammie, Tish, Andy . . . almost everyone in the Service Club is coming. Today we've just gotta finish these darn wreaths so we can start selling them." She pulled the plastic drop cloths off a table stacked with the fresh evergreen wreaths the club had made the week before.

The others drifted in, ignoring the wreaths but attacking the refreshments. Sonja found Nguyen and asked about Tim Powell.

"The decathlon team calls him 'El braino,' " said Nguyen. "All I know is that he always has the right answer. He doesn't do anything but hit the books—some days he doesn't even speak to people. If he can pull us through this month's county finals, we're in line for some major scholarship money, plus a bonus for the school. Then on to the finals and even bigger winnings."

"Okay, okay—enough gossip. Let's get serious, guys," said Donna, stuffing one last brownie into her mouth. "This is ribbon day. Leslie got over a hundred yards of ribbon donated, so we're going to make those bows and finish this project."

Will joked, "Do we each get to take one home?"

"Sure," said Barb, the treasurer, "just give me a ten and it's yours. Do you realize that with most everything donated to us, we'll clear almost a thousand dollars? So we can use some of that for the children's hospital Christmas party."

"I can't tie bows," protested Sonja.

"Then we'll tie them and you wire them in place," Donna answered. Sonja was a good friend, but she was also a complainer.

Soon the assembly line was set up, with Leslie cutting ribbon, many tying the big bows, Sonja affixing them, and Will putting the hanging hooks on the back. By 5:30, Donna's father came home from work and offered to drive a carload of kids to their houses.

"Anything to get this project out of my basement," he teased as the group admired the completed wreaths.

Donna reminded them, "We're each responsible for selling three, so take your three with you now. I'll get the rest of them to the booth at school." She watched five kids with fifteen wreaths pile into the car, as others started to walk home or waited on the porch for their rides.

"Where's my mom? She's always late!" grumbled Sonja, standing at the living room window with Donna. "And how are you going to get all these wreaths to the booth at school? Certainly not on the bus!"

"Sometimes I take the morning school bus, but Dad drives me to school many days. He's agreed to take me in the car for the next few days until I can get all the wreaths there," said Donna.

But the next morning, the plan didn't work. The car made a croaking sound and then quit. Donna's folks dashed to catch the bus to take them downtown. Donna looked dejectedly at the car loaded with wreaths. What was she going to do? The sales booth at school was to open that day. Finally she figured she could carry ten wreaths to school by putting them in plastic grocery bags and hanging the bags on her arms.

Walking carefully on the icy sidewalk, she struggled to the corner just in time to see the school bus coming. As it slowed to a stop and she climbed on, Tim Powell raced out of his house and jumped aboard as the door closed. Donna decided that his system was to wait in the front window until he saw the bus—anything to avoid people, she thought.

When the bus reached the school, she gathered her load and was inching down the aisle when a voice said, "Let me help you with some of those."

Tim reached out and took most of them and carried them to the Service Club booth, walking slightly ahead of her. He was turning to leave when Donna asked, "Want to buy a wreath for the front door of your house?"

"Sorry, I don't like wreaths," he said and was gone.

"What was all that?" asked Sonja, who was there to man the booth the first hour. Donna smiled, remembering that Sonja had insisted on saying she would "woman" the booth first period when she didn't have a class.

"Nothing," said Donna, looking after Tim.

"Something's cooking. Tell me," demanded Sonja.

"Another time," said Donna. "I hope you sell lots of those wreaths—I have to get to class."

Donna was an average student, so she usually didn't see Tim at school, since he was in advanced placement classes. But at least she had now had one conversation with him.

Later that morning, she noticed an article in the school newspaper. There was a long interview and photo of each person on the decathlon team—except Tim. Aside from there being no picture, there was just one line of copy: "Tim Powell moved here from Florida last September and plans to go to college next fall." Nothing more.

At lunch Sonja pointed to the article and said, "They should have made him have his picture taken and describe his life, just like the others did." Donna just kept eating, and Sonja continued, "Donna, you ride the afternoon bus with him every day. You've just got to be more aggressive if you're interested in this guy."

Donna made a face. "Aggressive? And who said I was interested? I can't even get him to be civil. He makes sure that he's the last one to get on the bus and the first one to get off."

"So change that," said Sonja sharply.

That afternoon Donna sat in the first row of the bus—the place no one wanted to sit. But she did it so she could be first off the bus at her stop. And when Tim stepped down behind her, she said, "I read in the school paper that you're from Florida." He said nothing, but she was determined not to be put off easily. Taking Sonja's suggestion, she continued, "You've been used to warm weather, so how do you think you're going to like Christmas with snow and freezing temperatures?"

They were standing at the corner across from his house, and he looked at her as if she were from another planet. "I don't mind the weather," he said, "but I hate Christmas." Before she could recover from her surprise and his rudeness, he was across the street and up the stairs of his house—gone from sight. She walked down the block to her house, wondering what would make a person hate Christmas, her most favorite holiday.

The next day she walked from assembly with Sonja and Nguyen. Sonja insisted on knowing what had happened, so Donna told her that she and Tim had now had a second conversation.

"Not really a conversation," she added. "He just informed me that he hates Christmas."

"I told you he was different," said Nguyen. "His decathlon tutor is that English teacher, Seth Thomas. Thomas is really great and prepares us for the decathlon by making long lists of typical questions—then he rapid-fire quizzes us. But he's especially working with Tim on lit, same as Craig Levy does for me in history."

"Sounds tedious to me," commented Sonja. She pointed to a poster announcing the holiday dance in the gym. "Do you realize that your decathlon semi-final is that Friday—the same day as the dance?"

"Sure do," said Nguyen. "I'm coming to the dance to celebrate our big win."

By the end of the week, the wreaths had sold so well that the Service Club knew it had enough money to cover the Christmas party they were giving for the children's hospital and as well as funds for their other projects.

For the party, Sammie and Sonja were in charge of the Christmas cupcakes, and Sonja let everyone know just how much work that was. Barb and Leslie were wrapping small gifts for each child, and Nguyen was producing on his computer an illustrated Christmas song sheet for each child. But they were one person short—the one to wear the Santa suit and give out candy canes. All the other Service Club guys would be taking part in a basketball game that afternoon.

"I guess you'll have to be Santa as well as leading the carols," said Donna to Nguyen.

"Me?" he asked, laughing. "A Vietnamese Santa? I think that's carrying my Americanization too far. Besides, I'm too short for that Santa suit. You need a tall guy."

Sonja teased Donna: "Get Tim Powell to be the Santa. For sure he won't be at the basketball game."

"I know you think that's a joke," said Donna, "but that's exactly what I plan to do!"

Donna told her father not to drive her to school the next morning. She waited in the cold at the bus stop and, like clockwork, as the bus was about to leave, Tim ran from his house and hopped aboard. He sat in the back, in a row to himself. Undaunted, Donna got up from her seat and walked back to sit next to him.

"There's something I'd like you to do for the Service Club," she began. She told about the party at the hospital and how they needed a Santa.

"I'm sorry," he said, "but I can't do it. I'm not a ho-ho-ho type of person, and as I told you before, I hate Christmas."

Donna bit her lip and pursued the subject. "I don't think you mean that. I bet your folks celebrate Christmas. Don't you have a Christmas tree? And gifts?"

"No folks, no Christmas tree, no gifts." He got up and moved to another seat.

Tim wasn't on the bus going home that afternoon, but she felt she should find him and apologize—for what, she wasn't sure—but she needed to know more about his anger about Christmas. Somehow she felt she had hurt him.

She got off at the corner and decided it wouldn't hurt to ring his doorbell and at least say something pleasant. She didn't like conversations that ended with someone walking away. She had her books on one arm and an extra wreath hung over the other arm. It was the very last one, and her father had said he'd buy it for the office if it didn't sell at school.

No one answered the doorbell. She was about to leave the front porch when the door opened and a sixtyish woman asked what she wanted.

"Is Tim home?" Donna asked. The woman explained that he was studying late at school.

"Oh yes," said Donna, "for the decathlon next week. You must be very proud of him."

Seeing her load of books, the woman asked if she'd like to come in. The house was furnished with antiques and books—actually more books than antiques.

They spoke a few moments about Tim's love of books and then the woman said, "Tim is my grandson, and I know that this decathlon is very important to him. He's working so hard, poor boy, pursuing every avenue to earn money for college. And he's going to need some scholarships to make it. You know he works every weekend at the Chevron station."

Donna didn't know that. "So he doesn't get to go to the school events on Saturday or to church on Sunday?"

Mrs. Powell said softly, "He hasn't been to church since his folks and his sister were killed by a drunk driver. That was last Christmas Eve."

Donna was stunned and could only say, "Oh my!"

Mrs. Powell continued, "I've tried everything to help him, but he won't talk about it at all. It's as if last Christmas was just wiped out of his mind."

"Well, I'd like to be his friend, but he doesn't seem to need a friend—or anyone," said Donna, rising to leave.

"Yes, he thinks he has to do it all himself. He loved his family so much—his dad was my only son—and now Tim finds it hard to get close to anyone. My minister has helped me a lot, but he says that it will just take more time for Tim. I feel so sad this year—there's not a bit of Christmas in this house. Tim is such a good boy, but he gets very sullen if I even mention putting up a tree."

Donna looked at the wreath. "Here, let me give this to you—it's an extra one, and I'd be so pleased if you'd take it for your front door."

Mrs. Powell hesitated, then smiled and said, "Well, that's very nice of you. I'd like that a lot."

Around eight o'clock that night, the Davis doorbell rang, and Mrs. Davis answered it. "Someone's here to see you, Donna," she called upstairs.

Donna was surprised to find Tim standing in the front hall. Then she noticed he was holding the wreath. "I'm bringing this back to you," he said, holding it out.

She put her hands behind her back, took a deep breath, and said boldly, "I can't take it. You need it. A wreath is a symbol of eternal life, and you need to think about that when you think about your family."

"What do you know about eternal life, and what do you know about my family?" he demanded angrily.

"I know that your folks and your sister would be very disappointed if they thought you commemorated their lives by hating Christmas. They enjoyed this Christmas celebration of love, and you're defaming it with your hate."

Tim's face grew red. "I don't need anyone to lecture me on religion!"

"No, you don't seem to need anyone for anything," she said in a loud tone that surprised even her.

"I have my priorities," he countered loudly.

"Well, you may be the smartest person at our school, but your priorities are all wrong. There are a few things even I could teach you," she shouted back.

"That will be the day," he said, storming out the door.

She noticed that he still had the wreath in his hand. And the next morning on the way to the bus she also noticed it was hung on his front door. She was so mad at him, she actually hoped she didn't see him running for the bus. She slid into a seat by the window and was surprised that a moment later he sat down next to her.

Looking directly at her, he said, "I'm sorry I shouted at you last night. Your folks must think I'm a jerk."

"Yes, they do," she said, smiling at him. She wondered if he ever smiled.

"It's just that Christmas is really hard for me. It used to be my favorite holiday. Now, I wish it could be over soon."

"It's the best time of the year for me. It's the foundation for the whole year that follows it," she said.

"Well, for me, last Christmas marked the end of many things I love. I just have to focus on my education. I want to be a writer, a poet, a teacher—I don't know—something that makes a difference to people. And I have to think about taking care of Gram. She's all that's left of my family."

"A poet! Who's your favorite?" she asked.

He didn't hesitate and said, "Probably Whittier."

"Wow, you won't believe this, but he's mine, too. I didn't even know he existed until I had a lit class this year."

"I think you're just humoring me by saying he's your favorite," he said, half-smiling. "Quote me something he wrote—anything."

She thought a moment, then shook her head.

"Gotcha. You don't even know anything about John Greenleaf Whittier."

"I do, too, but I don't think you'll like what I remember of his."

"Try me."

She said, "It's from his poem 'The Chapel of the Hermit.' "

"Yeah, I know that one."

"I bet you do because you're a hermit, too."

"Don't pick on me, just quote."

"Here goes," she said, concentrating hard and hoping she could remember the lines:

> "'O, sometimes gleams upon our sight,
> Through present wrong, the eternal right;
> And step by step, since time began,
> We see the steady gain of man.'

and woman," she added. "Now comes the part you need to hear:

> 'For all of good the past hath had
> Remains to make our own time glad.'"

She stopped and looked at him. "Don't you see? All the good things your parents taught you—the things they did with you—remain with you and can make the present happy."

He didn't answer, but he did give her a long look. It was time to get off the bus. He didn't speak but walked slowly next to her toward her classroom. When he stopped to leave her, he turned and said, "Thank . . . you."

All the rest of the week, they talked every day on the bus. He even met her each morning at the bus stop, and they talked while waiting in the cold. She told him about all the things her family did to celebrate the holidays. And little by little he began to remember some of his own family's Christmas traditions. Donna noticed that he no longer looked sad when they talked about Christmas. And his half smile was sometimes a full smile. And he often smiled at her!

Then one day, going home on the bus, he was back in his silent mood. She asked him if he was depressed about Christmas, but he brushed her off. Getting off the bus at the corner by his house, she decided to bring up a new subject.

"Did you know that you live in the former coach house of the Collins estate? Their big house at the end of the street was bulldozed about two years ago so that those six new houses could be built."

Tim seemed interested. "So I live in a little bit of history. Wasn't Collins governor?"

"Yes, and Dad says he was a good one. Even though his house was bulldozed, they didn't bulldoze all the good stuff he did."

Tim laughed, "I know—the Whittier line: 'All of good the past hath had remains to make our own time glad.' "

"Now," she said, "tell me what's bugging you this afternoon."

"It's the decathlon. My English tutor, Mr. Thomas, has had to go out of town suddenly on a family emergency, and there's no one to drill me. The other tutors are busy, and the team members are busy, so I'm on my own, I guess."

"How does he drill you?" she asked.

"Well, there are these long lists he's made up—pages and pages of authors and their writings. I guess I can study by myself. But it seems better when the questions are fired at you as they will be in the competition."

"Your grandmother can't do it?"

"She's taken a temporary Christmas sales job at one of the malls—she'll be working from two in the afternoon until ten most every night. I can't ask her to do more."

Donna touched his arm. "How about me? I can read, you know."

"Oh, that's nice, but I just can't be . . . beholden to anyone," he said slowly.

"Beholden! Where did you get that old-fashioned word! Do you really think it's bad to let someone do something for you?"

"Sure I do," he argued. "You get indebted to someone, and you have to pay them back! How would I ever pay you back?"

"Come on, Tim, trust a little. Let me help you—you can return the favor any time in the next hundred years—or never."

He ran his wool glove over his hair and said slowly, "I do need to get that scholarship so I can make something of myself—for me and for Gram." He paused, then looked at her and added, "I guess we can try it."

The next three afternoons they worked together. Donna's parents were impressed with their diligence and glad that Donna was learning so much about literature while drilling Tim. One night he stayed for supper and actually became quite comfortable with her folks. Another day when Sonja came over to help, Tim admitted it was getting to be fun.

"If you call this fun, I dread to think what you call work," Sonja snapped.

When Tim didn't remember an answer, Donna slipped the question back in again until he got it right. Donna never knew there were so many writers, so many books, so many poets and poems.

One afternoon they were alone studying at his house. Donna was sitting by the bookshelves where she noticed a framed photo of Tim with his sister and parents. She picked it up and looked at it.

"You must really love them," she said, scrutinizing each face in the picture.

"And I hate the driver who killed them," he said sharply. "He ended the lives of three good people, but the scum gets to live. How I hate him!"

Donna couldn't let that comment pass. "Just think how terrible he must feel. Every single day of his life he has to think about what he's done. He needs your love and your forgiveness."

"That sounds good, but I don't feel like forgiving him," said Tim tersely.

"Your mother is beautiful!" she commented.

Tim looked at Donna. "*Is* beautiful? I'd say *was*."

Donna smiled. "No, I'm sure she still is beautiful, doing beautiful things. And you probably have no idea of all the good things she did here. Like a pebble dropped in a pond, the good she did radiates outward—beyond what you can see. Have you ever thought about that?"

He made a face, but she pretended not to notice. "She wanted the best for you, so let's get back to these questions so you can get that scholarship."

"In a minute," said Tim, in a sudden softer tone. "Do you still need a Santa for the children's party?"

"We sure do. We were just going to do without one, but you know how little kids would love seeing a Santa."

"I guess I can do it, even with decathlon study," he said.

"Are you doing this just to pay me back for helping you study? If so, forget it. I want you to do it because you know it's a good thing to do and you want to do it."

"Okay, okay. I want to do it," he said. "You sure are reforming my bad character."

The party was that weekend. The gifts and cupcakes, the balloons and music, all brightened the children's hospital. But Tim was the biggest hit. Hidden behind costume and beard, he became a different person—funny, caring, gently hugging each child.

Even Sonja noticed it. "Who does he think he is, suddenly becoming the center of attention at our party?"

Nguyen couldn't help saying, "Sonja, sometimes you should just shut your mouth."

When Donna's dad came to pick up Tim and Donna after the party, he brought up the subject of Tim's education. "Are you good only in English? I have a co-worker at the office looking for someone good in math and tabulation—computer stuff."

Tim said he was in advanced placement math and competent on his PC.

Mr. Davis continued, "I was thinking about your having to work at that gas station for minimum wage both Saturday and Sunday. This could work out to be a six- to eight-month job that would take just your Saturdays and maybe earn you more than your present job. It might even be full-time in the summer. That could tide you over until you go off to college in the fall. And, as a full-time employee, there might be some other benefits—even some funds for tuition."

"You'd do this for me?" asked Tim in amazement. "Why?"

"You'd have to sell yourself, but you seem like a hard-working guy, your manners are pretty good, I can tell you're plenty smart, and my co-worker could use the help. Besides, my daughter says you're worth it." And so the deal was set. After an interview, Tim got the job and was to start after Christmas. But he had little time to think of his good fortune, since the decathlon semi-finals were the upcoming Friday.

At the end of school Thursday, Nguyen ran into Tim, Donna, and Sonja in the hall.

He said, "Well, this is the night we all get a good long rest, Tim. No burning the midnight oil. And remember, we're through about five, and the van will bring us back here by seven, just in time for the dance."

Sonja smirked, "Tim at a dance? What's this silly world coming to?"

Donna said softly, "I'd like you to come, Tim. It's not a date event; everyone's just going to be here having fun."

"I don't think I will. I don't even know how to dance."

"Well, at least the van will stop at school. Think about coming in for a moment before going home," said Donna.

"Yeah," said Sonja, "we'll speak to you, win or lose." Donna gave Sonja a nudge with her elbow, but Sonja nattered on. "Just think, in twenty-four hours it will be over and you can be an ordinary person again—whatever ordinary is to you." Donna decided there was little hope for Sonja.

On the bus going home, Tim and Donna didn't talk. Then Tim suddenly grasped her hand so hard that she could feel his tenseness. He didn't speak.

"You're going to do it," she said. "You're well prepared. Besides, I'm pulling for you." When they got off the bus, he took her hand more gently, and they walked down to the end of Collins Avenue and back, talking about the day ahead, but most of all, not wanting to part from each other.

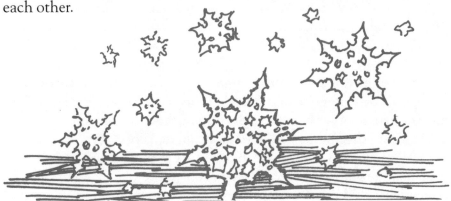

Friday dawned, cold and blustery, with snow both falling and swirling. Despite the gray morning, everyone at school was excited—first cheering the decathlon team as they left in the school van, then working on the preparations for the dance that evening, and finally thinking about two solid weeks of vacation for Christmas and time for just doing nothing. For Donna, the clock seemed to creep through the day.

Sonja noticed. "You really like this guy!"

"Yes, I do," said Donna. "He's becoming very special—and we're good for each other. He knows more about facts and figures and deep concepts than I do. And I know more about how to enjoy life and get along with people than he does. We're each teaching the other."

"I understand. How cute!" said Sonja sarcastically. Donna didn't say anything more but decided that Sonja did not understand this at all.

Sonja had permission to use her mother's car that evening, and she picked up Donna. At the dance, everyone was anticipating the team's return, and all eyes turned toward the big gym doors each time they clanked open.

The gym actually looked pretty. Around the sides of the room were evergreen Christmas trees that would be part of a drawing to be held at eleven o'clock. Cut-outs of giant snowflakes hung from the ceiling, hiding the basketball back boards. And everyone was in stocking feet so the gym floor wouldn't be marred by heel marks. A mirrored silver ball sent light to every corner of the room as the DJ played music. The teachers ignored the dance floor and hovered over the snack table, especially watching the punch to make sure no one tried to "improve" on it.

After many false alarms, the doors of the gym finally opened wide, and in walked the team and the faculty who'd accompanied them. No one could tell from their faces what had happened, but it looked pretty grim.

Nguyen took over the microphone. "Ladies and gentlemen—and teachers." Everyone laughed. "First the bad news: At the end of the competition, we were asked the final question. We bombed." Everyone groaned. "Now the good news: That meant it was a tie, and each team would get five more questions." Everyone cheered. "Of the first four questions, they got three right and one wrong, so did we, so it came down to the very last question. It was on literature. That, of course, is Tim Powell's specialty. Where's Tim?" Someone pushed Tim forward.

"They missed their question, and so Tim had to answer it right for us to win. He thought for so long, I thought his mind had turned to mush. The question was 'Who wrote "Maude Muller"?'"

A student called out: "Why should I write her, I don't even know her!" A few of the more literary inclined students laughed.

Nguyen continued, "You know the line from 'Maude Muller': 'For all sad words of tongue or pen, The saddest are these: It might have been!' And the poet is—tell them Tim!"

Tim, now pushed against his will to the edge of the stage, turned and said confidently, "It was John Greenleaf Whittier."

The crowd roared and applauded. Nguyen thanked the team for their efforts and the teachers for their support, wished the team well with their scholarships, and said that the school would use the bonus grant for new library books.

Tim moved away from the stage toward the door, but Donna found him and threw her arms around his neck. "You did it. You and our poet John Greenleaf Whittier did it!"

"And you did it, too!" he said, putting his arms around her.

"Then you must be beholden to me," she said coyly.

"But you said one doesn't always have to pay back."

She countered, "True, you don't—unless you really want to. And I want you to pay me back by dancing just one dance before the van takes you home."

The faculty had talked the DJ into playing one slow set. As Donna and Tim walked onto the dance floor, the lyrics began: "I'm dreaming of a white Christmas. . . . "

"Remember, I don't know how to dance," Tim protested.

"Then, for a change, I'll teach you something." She took his arm and placed it around her, then she put her hand in his. "Now, just listen to the music and move with it."

It wasn't as difficult as he'd thought it would be. And holding her in his arms was nice, too. Lots of kids on the dance floor slapped him on the back and said things like "Way to go, Tim." This school dance stuff wasn't half bad either, he thought. Forget the van, he'd stay.

At 10:45 the DJ asked all the people to get out their ticket stubs for the Christmas tree drawing. Twelve lucky people would take home a tree to trim. The first eleven winners were quickly drawn. But when the twelfth was called, no one responded.

"Where's your ticket stub?" Donna asked.

"I don't know, I guess I stuffed it in some pocket," he said fumbling. "Here it is."

Tim was winner number twelve, and as he stepped forward to claim the tree, Donna said, "I suppose you don't want it."

"Well, I could take it home—Gram would like it. But I don't know how to get it there."

Sonja came over to congratulate him and to ask Donna if she was ready to go. "Come on, Tim, I'll give you a lift, and we'll rope your tree on top of the car." As Nguyen, Will, and Barb were helping tie the tree on the car roof, Sonja volunteered: "We'll help you decorate it. Do you have any ornaments?"

"Sorry, we got rid of them when we moved," said Tim.

"That's okay," said Sonja. "My mom wanted a tree with all blue balls on it this year. We'll stop at my house and get our regular ornaments—I'll loan them to you for a few weeks."

Donna nudged Tim, "That way you can be beholden to her, too." When Donna thought about this offer of Sonja's, she decided that there was some kindness in Sonja—and perhaps some hope for her after all.

Tim had never seen so many people in his living room. Gram just sat in a chair and watched the fastest and funniest tree-trimming party she'd ever seen. She didn't mind that they ate almost all the Christmas cookies she'd baked.

After everyone left, Gram and Donna and Tim sat in the living room and looked at the lighted tree. It was certainly Christmas once more. Some of the sorrow and hate, the loneliness and fear, had been wiped away.

"I'm just itching to cook a southern Christmas feast," said Gram. "Would you and your folks join us on Sunday night?" Donna said she'd check but was quite sure they could come.

Later, when Tim walked Donna back home, he said, "I'll miss talking with you on the bus—two whole weeks and no bus trips together."

He looked so unhappy that Donna laughed. "Well, I am right across the street. You can come over any time you want."

"But I don't need to be drilled on lit any more," he protested.

"Yea, but I'll give you lessons on dancing and sledding and cookie baking and how to have fun."

"Well," he said slowly, "I'll come as long as you don't remind me of how beholden I am to you!"

He laughed and kissed her on the forehead. She laughed and kissed him on the mouth. And then he kissed her several times more, but not on the forehead.

For the boy who hated Christmas, these kisses were the beginning of a new tradition. He thought of his family and how they would have liked Donna. He thought of going to Donna's house every day for the two weeks of vacation. He thought of college and of the years that would follow. And all those thoughts made him smile. Yes, with Donna's help, Christmas might once more be his favorite holiday.

All the way down Collins Avenue and right in his front door, he whistled a Christmas carol.

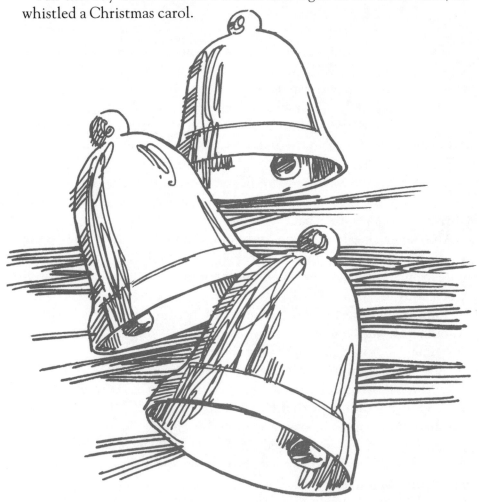

The Christmas Story
at Your House

"Christmas in France," by F. Méaulle, 1875.

Chapter Eight

The Christmas Story at Your House

Including the Best Story of All as Told in the Bible

Before this wondrous story, let's talk about the one Christmas decoration that is more important than a tree or a Santa or a wreath. It is a crèche. Whether it is called a crèche, a nativity scene, a cradle scene, a manger setting, or a tableau, the representation of the setting for Jesus' birth is always a memorable part of Christmas. The story that leads up to this cradle scene is one that many families cherish, and the telling of the story is their most treasured Christmas tradition.

If your family doesn't have a crèche, consider getting one. It will be a favorite part of your home's Christmas decorations and the focal point of your storytelling.

Crèches come in all varieties. Some are as simple as paper cut-outs; others are made of plastic, china, or wood. The figures are available in the traditional dress of Bible times, or in clothing typical of various nationalities.

You can spend as much or as little on a crèche as you wish. Many families have handed down their porcelain or wood crèches from one generation to another. If this is your plan, look for a sturdy one. The tableau usually consists of these pieces: the holy family with infant Jesus lying in the manger, shepherds and sheep, three kings, and a stable background. Sometimes there are other farm animals, too. And some sets feature an angel proclaiming the good news.

If you decide to buy a crèche, go as a family to purchase it. This can be the beginning of your month-long Christmas celebration.

Rather than setting up all the crèche pieces at one time, try reading the story and adding the characters as they appear in the text. This is especially intriguing for children, who like to unwrap the figures and put them in place. When you pack up your crèche after the holiday season, wrap carefully and label each character—that way you'll be ready for the next year.

In other chapters of this book, the crèche is referred to many times, especially in chapter 1, where it is the focal point of a storytelling session each Sunday during the holiday season. The story below notes which pieces to set up each week.

Here, then, are selections from the King James Version of the Bible. Although they are separated into five sections (to tie-in with the four Sundays before Christmas plus Christmas Eve), all of the story can be read at one time if you wish.

Chapter and verse citations are given at the beginning of each section, so you can easily use another version of the Bible if you prefer.

The First Sunday of December:
The Prophecy of Jesus' Coming

(Micah 5:2; . . . Isaiah 40:1-5; . . . Isaiah 9:2, 6-7)

Thou, Bethlehem Ephratah, though thou be little among the thousands of Judah, yet out of thee shall he come forth unto me that is to be ruler in Israel.

Comfort ye, comfort ye my people, saith your God. Speak ye comfortably to Jerusalem, and cry unto her, that her warfare is accomplished, that her iniquity is pardoned. . . .

The voice of him that crieth in the wilderness, Prepare ye the way of the LORD, make straight in the desert a highway for our God. Every valley shall be exalted, and every mountain and hill shall be made low: and the crooked shall be made straight, and the rough places plain: And the glory of the LORD shall be revealed, and all flesh shall see it together: for the mouth of the LORD hath spoken it.

The people that walked in darkness have seen a great light: they that dwell in the land of the shadow of death, upon them hath the light shined. . . .

For unto us a child is born, unto us a son is given: and the government shall be upon his shoulder: and his name shall be called Wonderful, Counsellor, The mighty God, The everlasting Father, The Prince of Peace. Of the increase of his government and peace there shall be no end, upon the throne of David, and upon his kingdom, to order it, and to establish it with judgment and with justice from henceforth even for ever. The zeal of the LORD of hosts will perform this.

Things to Talk About and Do

Who made the prophecy of Jesus' coming?
What does the word *messiah* mean?
Why were the people waiting for a Messiah, or Savior?
What were some of his other titles?
On a map, locate the cities of Bethlehem and Jerusalem.
Was Bethlehem a famous town at the time of Jesus' birth?

The Crèche:

Place the stable on a table or shelf in readiness for next week's reading.

The Second Sunday of December:
The Story of Mary and Joseph

(Matthew 1:18-23; . . . Luke 2:1, 3-7)

Now the birth of Jesus Christ was on this wise: When as his mother Mary was espoused to Joseph, before they came together, she was found with child of the Holy Ghost. Then Joseph her husband, being a just man, and not willing to make her a public example, was minded to put her away privily. But while he thought on these things, behold, the angel of the Lord appeared unto him in a dream, saying, Joseph, thou son of David, fear not to take unto thee Mary thy wife: for that which is conceived in her is of the Holy Ghost. And she shall bring forth a son, and thou shalt call his name JESUS: for he shall save his people from their sins. Now all this was done, that it might be fulfilled which was spoken of the Lord by the prophet, saying, Behold, a virgin shall be with child, and shall bring forth a son, and they shall call his name Emmanuel, which being interpreted is, God with us.

And it came to pass in those days, that there went out a decree from Caesar Augustus, that all the world should be taxed. . . . And all went to be taxed, every one into his own city. And Joseph also went up from Galilee, out of the city of Nazareth, into Judaea, unto the city of David, which is called Bethlehem; (because he was of the house and lineage of David:) To be taxed with Mary his espoused wife, being great with child. And so it was, that, while they were there, the days were accomplished that she should be delivered. And she brought forth her firstborn son, and wrapped him in swaddling clothes, and laid him in a manger; because there was no room for them in the inn.

Things to Talk About and Do

What is the Holy Ghost?
What does the name Emmanuel mean?
Why did Mary and Joseph have to go to Bethlehem?
Who was Caesar Augustus?
Who is the David that Joseph was related to?

In what ways was the stable a better place to have a baby than an inn?

On a map, find the city of Nazareth.

The Crèche

Place the figures of Mary and Joseph in the stable.

The Third Sunday of December:
The Story of the Shepherds

(Luke 2:8-18, 20)

And there were in the same country shepherds abiding in the field, keeping watch over their flock by night. And, lo, the angel of the Lord came upon them, and the glory of the Lord shone round about them: and they were sore afraid. And the angel said unto them, Fear not: for, behold, I bring you good tidings of great joy, which shall be to all people. For unto you is born this day in the city of David a Saviour, which is Christ the Lord. And this shall be a sign unto you; Ye shall find the babe wrapped in swaddling clothes, lying in a manger. And suddenly there was with the angel a multitude of the heavenly host praising God, and saying, Glory to God in the highest, and on earth peace, good will toward men. And it came to pass, as the angels were gone away from them into heaven, the shepherds said one to another, Let us now go even unto Bethlehem, and see this thing which is come to pass, which the Lord hath made known unto us. And they came with haste, and found Mary, and Joseph, and the babe lying in a manger. And when they had seen it, they made known abroad the saying which was told them concerning this child. And all they that heard it wondered at those things which were told them by the shepherds. . . . And the shepherds returned, glorifying and praising God for all the things that they had heard and seen, as it was told unto them.

Things to Talk About and Do

Why do you think that simple shepherds were the first to visit the Christchild?

Do angels ever talk to us today?

Memorize these famous words said by the angel: "Glory to God in the highest, and on earth peace, good will toward men."

The Crèche

Add the figures of the shepherds and the animals to the scene.

The Fourth Sunday of December: The Story of the Kings

It should be noted here that the kings' arrival was actually later—January 6. But common practice is to include them in the scene at this time. If your family celebrates Epiphany, you will have another occasion to talk about your crèche, and you may wish to add the wise men at that time, rather than now.

(Matthew 2:1-12)

Now when Jesus was born in Bethlehem of Judaea in the days of Herod the king, behold, there came wise men from the east to Jerusalem, Saying, Where is he that is born King of the Jews? for we have seen his star in the east, and are come to worship him. When Herod the king had heard these things, he was troubled, and all Jerusalem with him. And when he had gathered all the chief priests and scribes of the people together, he demanded of them where Christ should be born. And they said unto him, In Bethlehem of Judaea: for thus it is written by the prophet, And thou Bethlehem, in the land of Juda, art not the least among the princes of Juda: for out of thee shall come a Governor, that shall rule my people Israel. Then Herod, when he had privily called the wise men, inquired of them diligently what time the star appeared. And he sent them to Bethlehem, and said, Go and search diligently for the young child; and when ye have found him, bring me word again, that I may come and worship him also. When they had heard the king, they departed; and, lo, the star, which they saw in the east, went before them, till it came and stood over where the young child was. When they saw the star, they rejoiced with exceeding great joy.

And when they were come into the house, they saw the young child with Mary his mother, and fell down, and worshipped him: and when they had opened their treasures, they presented unto him gifts; gold, and frankincense, and myrrh. And being warned of God in a dream that they should not return to Herod, they departed into their own country another way.

Things to Talk About and Do

Herod, the king, ruled Israel on behalf of what country?

From where did the kings come?

How do you know the kings were aware of the prophecy?

Why was Herod interested in the baby Jesus?

We know what gold is, but what were the gifts of frankincense and myrrh?

What wise thing did the wise men do after honoring Jesus?

The Crèche

Add the figures of the three kings to the manger scene.

Christmas Eve

(Luke 2:40; Matthew 4:23-24; Matthew 5:2, 16; Matthew 10:8; John 13:34; John 21:25; Revelation 19:6, 16)

And the child grew, and waxed strong in spirit, filled with wisdom: and the grace of God was upon him.

And Jesus went about all Galilee, teaching in their synagogues, and preaching the gospel of the kingdom, and healing all manner of sickness and all manner of disease among the people. And his fame went throughout all Syria: and they brought unto him all sick people that were taken with divers diseases and torments, and those which were possessed with devils, and those which were lunatic, and those that had the palsy; and he healed them.

And he opened his mouth, and taught them, saying, . . . Let your light so shine before men, that they may see your good works, and glorify your Father which is in heaven.

Heal the sick, cleanse the lepers, raise the dead, cast out devils: freely ye have received, freely give.

Love one another; as I have loved you, that ye also love one another.

And there are also many other things which Jesus did, the which, if they should be written every one, I suppose that even the world itself could not contain the books that should be written.

And I heard as it were the voice of a great multitude, and as the voice of many waters, and as the voice of mighty thunderings, saying, Alleluia: for the Lord God omnipotent reigneth. Let us be glad and rejoice, and give honour to him . . . KING OF KINGS, AND LORD OF LORDS.

Things to Talk About and Do

Do you remember Joseph's occupation, which he taught to Jesus?
At about what age did Jesus begin his ministry?
How many miracles and healings by Jesus can you name?
What do you think was Jesus' greatest victory?

The Crèche

Add the figure of baby Jesus to the crèche. Now your nativity scene is complete.

The story of the birth and life of Jesus is the foundation for a happy and meaningful Christmas. His teachings set an example for the perfect life. How much happier would we all be, how much more peaceful the world would be, if we each honored him in both our words and our deeds.

Children and adults, those gathered in groups for Christmas, as well as those celebrating alone, can use this day to rededicate themselves to the principles of Jesus' teaching: to help ease the pain of the world, to love and care for one another, to put God first, and to be as pure and honest and perfect as we can possibly be . . . to go forward each day with hope, feeling the blessing of Jesus Christ, who gave his life for us.

These are not lofty, impossible-to-obtain attitudes. They are possible here and now. Why think of them only on Sunday or at Christmas? What is good should take precedence in our lives. Then every day can be as joyous as Christmas day.

Merry Christmas to you now—and every day!

Find Baby Jesus

CHARLES COX

A Bibliography of
Good Christmas
Literature

Always Christmas. Wilbur D. Nesbit. Chicago: Volland Company, 1920.

American Christmas. Edited by Webster Schott and Robert J. Myers. Kansas City: Hallmark Cards, Inc., 1965.

The Book of Christmas. New York: Reader's Digest Association, 1985.

Christmas. Better Homes and Garden. New York: Meredith Gardens, 1974.

Christmas. Leo Buscaglia. New York: Morrow, 1987.

Christmas. Barbara Heine Costikyan. New York: Pantheon, 1982.

Christmas All Through the House. J. B. Brimer. New York: Funk & Wagnalls, 1968.

Christmas Almanac. Gerard Del Re. New York: Doubleday, 1979.

Christmas at Bracebridge Hall. Washington Irving. New York: David McKay Company, 1962.

Christmas at Rancho Los Alamitos. Katharine B. Hotchkis. San Francisco: California Historical Society, 1957.

215

The Christmas Box. Eve Merriam. New York: Morrow, 1985.

A Christmas Carol. Charles Dickens. Various editions.

Christmas Crafts and Customs Around the World. Virginia Fowler. New York: Simon and Schuster, 1988.

Christmas Gems. Mable Hunter Hoggan. Minneapolis: Denison, 1950.

Christmas in the Forest. Jan Wahl. New York: Macmillan, 1970.

Christmas Joys. Joan W. Brown. New York: Doubleday, 1982.

The Christmas Mice. John W. White. Stillpoint, N.H.: Angel Food Books, 1984.

Christmas Plays and Programs. Aileen Lucia Fisher. Boston: Plays, Incorporated, 1960.

The Christmas Story. Edited by Marguerite Northrupe. New York: Metropolitan Museum of Art, 1966.

Christmas the World Over. Daniel J. Foley. Philadelphia: Chilton, 1963.

The Christmas Train. Ivan Gantschev. New York: Little Brown, 1984.

Christmas Treasures. Kansas City: Hallmark Cards, 1966.

The Donkey's Dream. Barbara Helen Berger. New York: Philomel, 1985.

An Early American Christmas. Tomie DePaola. New York: Holiday House, 1987.

The Family Christmas Tree Book. Tomie DePaola. New York: Holiday House, 1980.

Gus Was a Christmas Ghost. Jane Thayer. New York: Morrow, 1969.

The Joys of Christmas. Kathryn Jackson. New York: Golden Press, 1976.

The Little Drummer Boy. Katherine Kennicott Davis. New York: Macmillan, 1968.

Little Tree. e. e. Cummings. New York: Crown, 1987.

The Miracle of Christmas. Hallmark Cards, 1966.

The Night Before Christmas. Clement Clarke Moore. Various editions.

The Night Ride. Aingelda Ardizzone. New York: E. P. Dutton, 1975.

Noel's Christmas Secret. Gregoire Solotareff. New York: Farrar Straus Giroux, 1991.

An Old Fashioned Christmas. Paul Engle. New York: Dial Press, 1964.

The Oxford Christmas Book for Children. Roderick Hunt. London: Oxford University Press, 1981.

The Polar Express. Chris Van Allsburg. Boston: Houghton Mifflin, 1985.

Star in the East. Hans Holzer. New York: Harper & Row, 1968.

The Story of Christmas. Reginald John Campbell. New York: Macmillan, 1934.

The Substitute Guest. Grace L. Hill. Mattituck, N.Y.: Amereon Ltd., 1936.

The Tale of Three Trees. Angela E. Hunt. Batavia, Ill.: Lion, 1989.

The Tiniest Candle. Damon Younger. San Diego: Oak Tree, 1978.

Tree Full of Stars. Doris Grubb. New York: Scribner's, 1965.

The 12 Days of Christmas. Miles Hadfield. New York: Little, Brown, 1962.

"12 Days of Christmas." Jack Kent. Bergenfield, N.J. *Parent's Magazine*, 1973.

Why Christmas Trees Aren't Perfect. Richard H. Schneider. Nashville: Abingdon Press, 1988.

A Wreath of Christmas Legends. Phyllis McGinley. New York: Macmillan, 1967.

Index